THE CHAIN REACTION

Pioneers of Nuclear Science

THE CHAIN REACTION

Pioneers of Nuclear Science

KAREN FOX

Lives in Science

Franklin Watts
A Division of Grolier Publishing
New York • London • Hong Kong • Sydney
Danbury, Connecticut

For Dad,
who first taught me Newton's Laws

Cover design by Marie Greco Interior design by Molly Heron

Photographs ©: AIP Emilio Segre Visual Archives: 115; Archive Photos: 38 (Deutsche Presse Agentur), 86, 87, 125; Corbis-Bettmann: cover, right top, 12, 18, 21, 23, 53; Los Alamos National Lab: cover, 61; National Archives: 56 (Courtesy of USHMM Photo Archives), 80; Photo Researchers: 3, 5, 9, 27, 46, 64, 95, 110 (Michael Gilbert), 31 (SPL), 32 (Mary Evans Picture Library), 62 (Mark Marten), 65 (SPL), 41; UPI/Corbis-Bettmann: cover right center, cover right bottom, 47, 51, 66, 68, 75, 89, 91, 97, 105, 108.

Illustrations by Pat Rasch

Visit Franklin Watts on the Internet at:
http://publishing.grolier.com

Library of Congress Cataloging-in-Publication Data

Fox, Karen
    The chain reaction: pioneers of nuclear science / Karen Fox.
        p.   cm. — (Lives in science)
    Includes bibliographical references and index.
    Summary: Profiles seven people—including Marie Curie, Enrico Fermi, Robert Oppenheimer, and Andrei Sakharov—whose study of the atom has shaped the field of nuclear science during this century.
    ISBN 0-531-11425-2
    1. Nuclear physicists—Biography—Juvenile literature. 2. Nuclear physics—History—Juvenile literature. [1. Nuclear physicists. 2. Nuclear physics.]
    I. Title. II. Series.
    QC774.A2F69 1998
    539.7'092'2—dc21
    [B]   97-34769
                                                                  CIP
                                                                   AC

ACKNOWLEDGMENTS

*N*umerous people read early drafts and gave helpful comments, including Amber Scholtz, Lisa Seachrist, David Kestenbaum, and Spencer Weart, who heads the History Center of the American Institute of Physics. Most of the research for this book was done at the Niels Bohr Library at the American Center for Physics.

Much of this book was written in numerous coffee shops in the Washington, D.C., area with the almost constant companionship of Misha Strauss, who was alternately quietly supportive and totally distracting, but always an integral part of the process. (Hopefully baby Hannah subconsciously picked up some physics along the way!) I also wrote extensively in my home office—thank you to all four parents who helped get me into my new home. The rest of the book was written at Mom and Bill's, who have given me continual support and a place to hide when I need one. Lastly, thanks to Rebecka Peebles and Noah Schenendorf, just because.

CONTENTS

INTRODUCTION

*D*emocritus, an ancient Greek philosopher, believed that everything in the world was made up of tiny particles called *atoms*. According to his theory, water was made up of water atoms, stone was made up of stone atoms, and fire was made up of fire atoms. He used the term atom because it means "indivisible." Democritus believed that atoms were the smallest pieces of *matter* in the universe; they could not be divided into anything smaller.

In the 1800s, scientists proved that Democritus was partly right—everything *is* made up of atoms. In the early 1900s, however, scientists learned that Democritus was also partly wrong. Atoms are composed of even smaller *subatomic particles* called *electrons, protons,* and *neutrons*. Protons and neutrons make up the *nucleus*—the core of an atom. Electrons whiz around the nucleus.

The discovery of the nucleus has created a whole new branch of physics known as *nuclear science*. During the past century, the study of nuclear science has changed the world. The number of protons and neutrons in the nucleus determines whether an atom will be oxygen or lead or gold or any one of more than 100 other types of atoms. The ratio of subatomic particles in an atom's nucleus determines whether or not the atom will be radioactive. The nucleus even plays a key role in the process that keeps the sun burning.

Studying the nucleus has done more than just expand our scientific knowledge; it has also opened the door for new technology. The nucleus contains a huge amount of energy. This energy can be harnessed and used to help or to harm. It can be used to destroy cancer cells or to generate electricity. It can also be used to make the most powerful and deadly weapons ever imagined.

During World War II, scientists working for the United States government learned to manipulate the nucleus in order to assemble the world's first atomic bomb. After seeing the terrible effects of this bomb, people all over the world realized that, while the pursuit of knowledge is important, we must take care in how we put that knowledge to use.

This book profiles seven men and women who have made groundbreaking contributions to the field of nuclear science. It traces the history of the science from the discovery of radioactivity to the creation of the first nuclear bombs and the development of the current description of particles in the nucleus. The chronological order of the chapters will allow you to see the underlying thread that links all the research.

ONE "THE PATH OF A NEW SCIENCE"

Marie Curie and the Discovery
of Radioactivity

*M*arie Curie spent the winter of 1898 in a tiny, drafty shed. There was no insulation to keep out the cold, and the dilapidated roof hardly protected her from rain and snow. But she needed a place to do research and this was the only laboratory space she could find in Paris. Looking back, Marie claimed that some of the happiest days of her life were spent working in that small, run-down shed. It was the place where she and her husband, Pierre, discovered two new atoms.

Marie had such a difficult time finding lab space and funding because her research was not fashionable. At that time, X rays were the most popular research topic. Their popularity was not confined to scientists' laboratories. They were also the chief form of wonder and entertainment at parties attended by upper-class Europeans. It was common for hostesses to set up machines that would make X-ray images of their guests' hands.

*The cold, dilapidated shed where Marie Curie
did her first research.*

Marie was not interested in X rays, but she was intrigued by the research of a scientist named Henri Becquerel. While investigating the source of X rays, Henri discovered that a mineral called uranium gave off a whole new kind of invisible ray. Henri had no idea how important these mysterious rays would turn out to be. It was Marie who used them to make one of history's most important scientific discoveries.

Marie wanted to solve the puzzle that Henri Becquerel's finding created. She began her investigation by checking to see if any other material gave off this type of ray. She and Pierre built a machine to measure the rays and placed it in an old wooden crate. The couple was actually measuring what they called the *radioactivity* of the minerals.

Marie tested mineral after mineral without success. Finally, she found her answer in a brown powder called pitchblende. She knew that pitchblende contains a small amount of uranium, so she expected to see some radioactive rays. She was shocked, however, by the results of her tests. How could so much radioactivity come from the uranium in pitchblende?

She later wrote, "There must be something else radioactive inside the pitchblende besides uranium. . . . My husband agreed with me and I urged that we search at once for this hypothetical substance. [In the beginning,] neither of us could foresee that this work [would lead us to] a new [branch of] science."

Marie and Pierre forged that new scientific path together. They worked side by side in Marie's tiny makeshift laboratory. Marie removed radioactive materials from pitchblende samples, and Pierre studied their properties. Marie spent hours hovering over boiling kettles—stirring and stirring with an iron bar, trying to extract the mysterious new material.

Marie and Pierre started out with a ton of pitchblende and ended up with only trace quantities of the new material. This small amount was all the Curies needed, however. It didn't take long to realize that they had isolated two brand-new radioactive atoms. They named one polonium, after Poland—Marie's beloved homeland—and the other radium.

At the time that the Curies made their discovery, scientists had already identified about seventy different types of atoms. They suspected that there might be others, but were not sure how to go about looking for them. Marie and Pierre's research offered a solution— search for radioactivity and see what you find.

The discovery of polonium and radium drew attention to the Curies. Scientists all over Europe began to study radioactivity. Soon, Curie rays were the fashionable topic of discussion at upper-class parties. They were even more popular than X rays!

Originally, scientists thought the most important thing about radioactivity was its usefulness in detecting new types of atoms. But the Curies' research showed that radioactive rays weren't just heat or energy released from the surface of a substance. The radioactivity was coming from deep within the atoms that made up the substance. This finding was the first step along the road to understanding the structure of the atom.

YOUNG MARIE CURIE

Marie Curie was born Marya Sklodowska on November 7, 1867. She was the fifth child of Vladyslav and Bronislawa Sklodowska. Her parents were both middle-class schoolteachers. The family lived under the strict rules of Russian-occupied Poland.

According to Russian law, children and their families could be punished if they were caught speaking Polish to one another. Refusing to let their culture die, Polish teachers secretly taught their language and customs to the students. This was a tricky endeavor because at any point a Russian inspector could pop in to check up on the lessons.

Little Marya was shy and afraid of the inspectors. Nonetheless, her teachers knew that she spoke Russian beautifully and always called on her to recite lessons for the inspectors. Marya wanted to run away and hide, but instead she would stand up and bravely recite Russian history or poetry as she was asked. Later in life, Marie blamed her fear of public speaking on these childhood experiences.

When Marie was just 15 years old, she graduated from high school. She was first in her class. As a female in turn-of-the-century Poland, the choices for her future were limited. Warsaw University would not accept women students. She could get married, but she did not fit her society's ideal of a marriageable young woman. She could teach at private schools as her mother had done. Or, she could go to college abroad. Marie had her heart set on furthering her education.

Even though traveling abroad cost more than her family could afford, Marie would not give up her dream. She and her older sister Bronia made a plan. Bronia would leave for Paris and begin her education while Marie worked to support her. When Bronia was finished with school and earning a salary, it would be Marie's turn to go to college. With visions of the university education ahead of her, Marie took a post as governess.

Late at night, when the children were asleep, Marie studied on her own. Sometimes she would read three or four books at a time! Some of these books discussed the basic principles of physics.

At that time, scientists agreed that everything in nature was made of atoms. They believed that the atom couldn't be broken up into anything smaller. Close to seventy different types of atoms had been discovered. (Each different kind of atom is called an *element*.) About 20 years earlier, in 1869, a Russian chemist named Dmitri Ivanovich Mendeleev had drawn the first table of elements in order of weight— from hydrogen, the lightest atom, all the way up to lead, which Mendeleev thought was the heaviest atom.

When Mendeleev began to organize the elements into a table, he noticed some patterns. Certain characteristics appeared in a predictable order. For example, in the lighter atoms, every eighth element was a gas that didn't mix with other elements. Mendeleev also realized that the patterns weren't quite perfect. The only way to perfect them was to incorporate some extra imaginary elements. Mendeleev predicted that these extra elements weren't imaginary at all. He thought they were elements that hadn't been discovered yet. Little did Marie know that she was destined to make some of those discoveries.

MARIE CURIE GOES TO PARIS

In 1891, 8 years after her graduation from high school, Marie received a letter from her sister Bronia inviting her to Paris. She arrived in France just a few weeks before fall classes began at the Sorbonne.

Marie lived alone in Paris. She had to walk up six flights of stairs to reach her dark, cold apartment. Sometimes she had to pile all her clothes on the bed to keep warm at night. The water in her washbasin often froze. But Marie was happy there. In her autobiographical notes she said, "I was entirely absorbed in the joy of learning and understanding. . . . This life had a real charm for me. It gave me a very precious sense of liberty and independence."

Marie was one of just twenty-three women out of the 1,800 students in the Science Department at the Sorbonne, but this didn't bother her. She became consumed by her studies. In 3 years she earned a Master's

Degree in physics, graduating first in her class. A year later she earned a Master's Degree in mathematics. That time she placed second in her class.

Marie worked so hard that she had no time to make friends. She may not have been attractive to men who were looking for a "typical" French wife, but her intelligence and hard work made her very attractive to Pierre Curie. Pierre was already a well-known scientist in Paris who didn't think he'd ever meet a woman of genius—until he met Marie.

Marie and Pierre were married in 1895. They were a perfectly matched pair—both were obsessed with science and with working in the laboratory. They were definitely not an average French couple. They worked together in the little shack, and Marie also helped Pierre prepare lectures for his students. They were very busy, but they still managed to find time to start a family. On September 12, 1897, Marie gave birth to a baby girl, Irène.

Marie faced the same problems that working mothers face today. She wrote in autobiographical notes, "It became a serious problem—how to take care of our little Irène and of our home without giving up my scientific work? Such a renunciation would have been very painful to me, and my husband would not even think of it; he used to say that he had got a wife made expressly for him to share all his preoccupations. Neither of us would contemplate abandoning what was so precious to both."

As soon as she had recovered from childbirth, Marie was back in her lab and ready to start work on her Ph.D. It was just about a year after Irène's birth that the Curies discovered the two new elements—polonium and radium.

Marie, Irène, and Pierre Curie in 1898

They were working so hard that their friends worried about them. They were always tired and Pierre's legs ached constantly. Marie lost 10 pounds (4.5 kg) in the 5 years following their discovery of polonium.

In a letter to the couple, one friend wrote, "You must not think of science every instant of your life, as you are doing. You must allow the body to breathe. You must sit down in peace at your meals and swallow them slowly, keeping away from discussion of distressing or dispiriting events. You must not read or talk physics while you are eating."

The poor health of both Curies may have been the result of more than simple exhaustion, however. Today, we know that large doses of radioactivity can be poisonous, and we suspect the Curies' health was affected by working with radioactivity every day. In fact, Pierre purposely exposed himself to radioactivity.

On one occasion, he placed a piece of barium against his arm and left it there for 10 hours. At first, his skin was only slightly red and irritated, but soon the rash got much worse. Within days, it was noticeably redder. Then a crust formed, and an open wound developed. It took almost 3 months for the wound to heal, and even then it left behind a spot of gray skin. Still, the Curies were so excited about their work that they didn't consider the dangers of radioactivity.

Today, doctors know that people should not be exposed to too much radioactivity. In the early 1900s, however, when everyone was swept up by the excitement of these brand new radioactive rays, people thought radium could cure any sickness. They even thought it could grow hair on a bald man's head!

𝓜ORE ACCOMPLISHMENTS FOR MARIE CURIE

Marie had discovered two new elements, written numerous scientific papers, and created a new rage in Paris before she found the time to complete her Ph.D. When she finally met with her review committee, they said that no doctoral dissertation had ever made such a tremendous contribution to science.

Earning her Ph.D. was just the first in a series of momentous events for Marie. Perhaps the most important was the birth of her second child, Eve. While Marie may have written one of the most impressive dissertations ever, she was still a woman at a time when women were expected to single-handedly run the household. Tired and sick after childbirth, Marie took some time off from the lab.

Marie's womanhood once again became an issue when her name was suggested to the Nobel Prize committee. In 1902, both Marie and Pierre were nominated for the prize, but they did not win. In 1903, Pierre was nominated with Henri Becquerel. Why was Marie included one year and not the next?

When word leaked to Pierre that he had been nominated without Marie, he quickly sent off a letter to the committee: "If it is true that one is seriously thinking about me, I very much wish to be considered together with Madame Curie with respect to our research on radioactive bodies." In the end, both Curies and Henri Becquerel won the Nobel Prize in physics for their joint research on the radiation phenomena. Marie Curie became the first woman in history to receive a Nobel Prize.

The Curies no longer had any trouble getting money or lab space. The Sorbonne created a chair especially for Pierre, while Marie was named chief of his laboratory. France loved to talk about this non-traditional couple. The press wrote that the couple's working relationship was romantic. Traditionalists argued that the laboratory was no place for a woman, while feminists announced that Marie was a role model for women everywhere.

The shy Curies didn't enjoy being in the limelight. Marie wrote, "The overturn of our voluntary isolation was a cause of real suffering for us and had all the effect of disaster." Whether they liked it or not, the Curies had become two of the most well-known scientists of their day.

Unfortunately for Marie, she soon had to learn to bear the attention all by herself. In 1906, Pierre, lost in

Henri Becquerel, the French scientist who discovered radioactivity

thought, walked across a crowded street. He bumped into a moving horse-drawn carriage and fell. The driver frantically veered to the side, but could not avoid hitting Pierre. The back wheel ran over his head and killed him instantly.

*L*IFE WITHOUT PIERRE

Marie was devastated by Pierre's death. In a journal she wrote, "He is gone forever, leaving me nothing but desolation and despair." At first Marie though she could not continue as a scientist, but eventually she felt that working in the lab brought her closer to Pierre.

Marie also honored her husband's memory by taking over his professorship at the Sorbonne. On November 5, 1906, as the first female professor in the history of the school, Marie Curie walked to the front of a Sorbonne classroom. The room was packed—not only with students, but with upper-class society, the press, and even foreign celebrities. They had all come to see the great scientist on this historic occasion. Marie gazed out, took a deep breath, and picked up Pierre's lectures right where he had left off.

During those first years after Pierre's death, Marie's schedule was busier than ever. She took care of her daughters, taught at the Sorbonne, and, of course, kept up her work in the lab. She wanted to learn more about the elements she'd discovered and figure out where they fit into Mendeleev's table of the elements—now called the *periodic table.*

Elements in the periodic table are arranged by weight. To determine the appropriate spots for polonium and radium, Marie needed to figure out their molecular weight. Her research showed that polonium should be element 84 and radium should be 88. During this period, she worked very hard. She didn't eat or sleep enough, and occasionally she even fainted.

It was not until 4 years after Pierre's death that Marie began to take joy in life again. Suddenly, she had stopped wearing black and she was smiling more. Her friends could not imagine what had brought about the change.

One man, Paul Langevin, knew why Marie was happier. The two had become close in the years after Pierre's death. Marie needed a friend, and Paul was trapped in an abusive marriage. Their loneliness

Marie Curie working in her laboratory in 1905

brought them together. After several years of friendship, Marie and Paul decided to rent an apartment together. While Marie never admitted it, it seemed clear that they were having an affair.

It was around this time that Marie became the first woman ever to be nominated to the French Academy of Sciences. Once again her name was splashed across the front page of every newspaper. Some claimed that her scientific accomplishments entitled her to the nomination. Others argued that women should not be allowed into the academy. In the end, the naysayers won—the Academy voted 85 to 60 in favor of upholding the all-male tradition.

Nevertheless, Marie was unable to escape the limelight. Paul's wife, Jeanne Langevin, became aware of his affair. French society at the time expected wives to look the other way if their husbands had a mistress. But Marie Curie was not just any mistress. She was a world-renowned scientist and Paul was in love with her.

Jeanne hired someone to break into Marie and Paul's apartment and steal their love letters. With the incriminating letters in hand, Jeanne threatened to expose the couple to the Parisian press. It is likely that Jeanne blackmailed them, taking money in exchange for her silence. For some time Marie and Paul kept their relationship low-key. Eventually, however, Jeanne broke her silence and went to the press. Once again, Marie Curie's name found its way into the Parisian headlines. Only this time it was not as a national heroine.

As quickly as Marie had become the darling of Paris, she now became the outcast. She was described as a husband stealer, a bad mother, and a scientist whose work was overrated. One newspaper published Paul and Marie's love letters. Up until then, Marie could claim it was a big misunderstanding. But with the publication of the letters, everyone in Paris was convinced of her guilt. The morning the scandalous letters were exposed, a crowd of angry rioters stood outside her house yelling and throwing stones.

In 1911, in the middle of the scandal, the Nobel committee voted to award Marie a second Nobel Prize, this time for chemistry. They wanted to reward her for the work that had created a whole new branch of science.

Due to the scandal, a friend on the committee advised her not to accept the prize in person. This was a harsh blow, but Marie's pride made her determined. She insisted on going to Stockholm, Sweden, to receive the prize. In her acceptance speech, Marie said, "Radioactivity is a very young science. It is an infant that I saw being born, and I have contributed all my strength to raising it. The child has grown; it has become beautiful."

Marie's relationship with Paul ended soon after her acceptance of the Nobel Prize. Two years later, he returned to his wife.

Years after the breakup, fate drew their two families together. Having no knowledge of the old scandal, Marie's granddaughter fell in love with—and married—Paul's grandson. Jeanne Langevin attended the wedding.

THE END OF MARIE CURIE'S LIFE

As Marie grew older, she stopped doing research. She concentrated more on helping the students in her lab to raise funds and publicize the many benefits of science.

It was in the 1920s that scientists first became aware of the dangers of prolonged exposure to radioactivity. Radioactive rays pack a huge jolt of energy that can speed through the skin like a microscopic bullet. When the energy slams into the *molecules* of a cell it can damage or even destroy them. A radioactive substance can affect a cell from far away and in a very unpredictable manner, so it is easy to see why it took such a long time for people to realize the danger of radioactivity.

As time went on, the number of people who had become sick and died from exposure to radiation increased. In one well-known case, female factory workers used radioactive ink to paint glow-in-the-dark numbers on watch faces. To make a finer point on their brushes, they would put the bristles in their mouths after dipping them in the ink. The amount of workers who suffered from cancer as a result of this was astounding! It could not be denied any longer. In large doses, radioactivity was deadly.

When Marie was 67 years old, her body finally surrendered to years of radiation exposure and overwork. She died at dawn on July 4, 1934. In death, she joined her beloved Pierre once again. Her coffin was placed right on top of his.

TWO

"AT THE CREST OF THE WAVE"

Ernest Rutherford
Discovers the Nucleus

When Ernest Rutherford began studying science in the late 1800s, the atom seemed like a fortress. No one knew what was behind the walls. Ernest wanted to break down those walls and take a look inside. The weapon he chose was a type of radioactive ray that he had named alpha radiation. Alpha particles are big and heavy. Ernest used them like cannonballs. He shot them at atoms to break down the walls, and then studied the wreckage.

It's as if you had a car with a sealed hood. In order to find out how the engine was made, you could smash a cannonball into it so forcefully that the pieces of the engine would fly in all directions. Then you could sift through the debris and get a pretty good idea of what was under the hood.

The most interesting thing Ernest found was a hard little ball at the center of the atom. He named this ball the nucleus. Until then, most people had

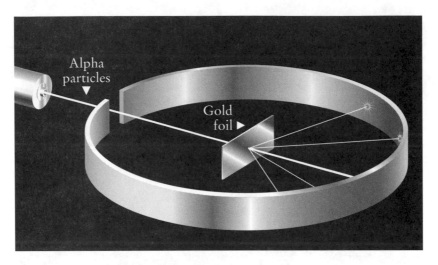

When Ernest Rutherford aimed a stream of alpha particles
at a piece of gold foil, most passed straight through but
a few bounced in different directions. Rutherford
theorized that something inside the gold atoms must
be deflecting the alpha particles. That "something"
was the gold atom's nucleus.

believed that the atom was a tiny fuzzy sphere with the consistency of a cloud.

Ernest discovered the nucleus when he was aiming alpha particles at a sheet of gold foil. Most of the time, the alpha particles zoomed right through the foil, but once in a while, something unexpected happened. Some of the alpha particles bounced back. It was one of the most incredible things Ernest had ever witnessed. "It's as if you fired a 15-inch shell at a piece of tissue paper, and it came back and hit you," he said. Ernest could not imagine what was happening. Then, an idea occurred to him—there must be something hard inside an atom.

Since most of the alpha particles passed straight through the foil, Ernest reasoned that the hard object must be much smaller than the whole atom. He was right. Today we know that if an atom were the size of a football stadium, the nucleus would be about the size of a marble.

Discovering the nucleus was the key to understanding how the atom is built. Scientists soon realized that it is the nucleus that makes one kind of atom different from another kind. The nucleus also determines whether an atom is radioactive and, thus, releases radioactive rays. Ernest's experiments had knocked down the walls of the mighty fortress and given scientists their first peek at the nucleus. Today, Ernest Rutherford is considered the father of nuclear science.

*Y*OUNG ERNEST RUTHERFORD

Ernest Rutherford was born in Nelson, New Zealand on August 30, 1871. His father, James Rutherford, was a farmer; his mother, Martha, was a school teacher. Ernest was the fourth of twelve children.

When he was 15 years old, Ernest won a scholarship to Nelson College Secondary School, a small private school that awarded only one scholarship to a rural child each year. Entire towns became caught up in the competition.

The pressure on Ernest was enormous. He took the test with the whole town whispering around him. One of his teachers stood over his shoulder and reported his progress to the community. The town gossips knew when he'd made a mistake long before Ernest did, but he wasn't distracted. He aced the test and won the scholarship.

It was at Nelson that he first learned about atoms. As he said later, "I was brought up to look at the atom as a nice hard fellow, red or gray in color, according to taste." Ernest was taught that the atom was a tiny, solid ball of material that could not be cut up into anything smaller.

He learned about the different elements of the periodic table and also discovered that scientists did not completely understand atoms and elements yet. For example, they knew that each element had a different weight, called an *atomic weight*. But they didn't know how differences in atomic weight were related to an element's physical properties. For instance, why was oxygen an invisible gas and gold a hard, shiny metal? Scientists were still looking for the answer to such questions.

Ernest graduated from high school at the head of his class and won a scholarship to the University of New Zealand. There he did research on radio waves and supported himself by teaching science and math at Christchurch Boys High School.

Since Ernest had no trouble understanding the sciences, it never occurred to him that his students might. Ernest didn't know how to make his lectures fun or interesting, or even simple. He stood in front of the classroom reeling off algebra equations and geometry proofs that were way over the boys' heads. They never understood any of it. Luckily for the students, though, Ernest also didn't take the time to check their homework. He usually gave them good grades no matter what they turned in.

During his years at the university, Ernest lived with Mrs. De Renzy Newton, a widow with four children. Her oldest daughter, Mary Georgiana, soon became a close friend. Ernest asked her to

Ernest Rutherford when he was 21 years old

marry him, but she refused, demanding that he fin-
ish his education without the distraction of a wife.
She did, however, agree to enter into a secret engagement and marry him when he received his degree.

Ernest applied for a research position at Cavendish
Laboratory at the University of Cambridge in England. Cavendish was considered the best place in the
world to do physics research. Ernest was working in
the garden when his mother brought him the letter
saying he'd been accepted. He threw down his spade
and said, "That's the last potato I'll dig!"

ERNEST RUTHERFORD DECIDES TO STUDY THE ATOM

During Ernest's second year at Cambridge, the world of physics changed dramatically. On Friday, April 29, 1897, J. J. Thomson, the head of Cavendish Laboratory, announced that atoms are not the smallest particles in the universe.

According to J. J., atoms have small, negatively charged particles inside them. These tiny particles always have the same mass and same charge, no matter which element they come from. J. J. called them "corpuscles," but today we call them electrons. Since the

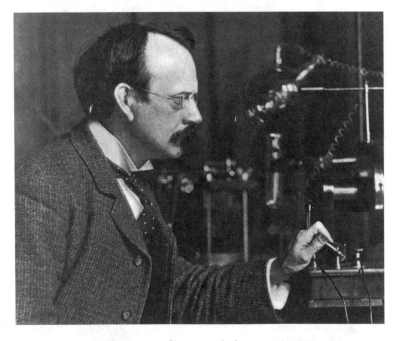

J.J. Thompson discovered electrons in 1897.

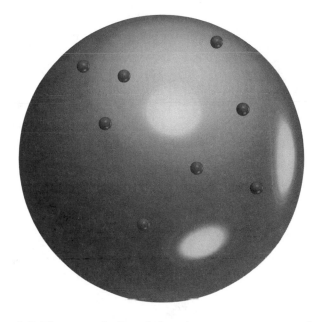

J. J. Thompson believed that electrons were scattered through an atom like seeds are scattered through a watermelon. Today we know that Thompson was wrong.

atom itself is neutral, Thomson believed all atoms must have an equal amount of positive charge to cancel out the electrons' negative charge. J. J. thought that electrons are scattered through an atom like seeds are scattered through a watermelon. He was the first scientist to suggest that atoms are made of smaller bits of matter.

J. J. Thompson's finding inspired Ernest to study the atom. Since the Curies were making headlines with their new radioactive atoms, Ernest decided to concentrate on these atoms, too. The Curies had found that radioactive rays are a by-product of a process occurring inside the atom. They had also discovered that the rays change the electrical conductivity of air as they pass through it.

By measuring this change, Ernest figured out how to track the rays as they move. He was surprised to discover that there are two types of rays. One kind is heavy and can be stopped by a very thin barrier of metal. The other kind can penetrate almost any material. He named the first kind *alpha rays* and the second kind *beta rays,* after the first two letters of the Greek alphabet.

ERNEST RUTHERFORD GOES TO CANADA

Ernest's work caught the attention of scientists at McGill University in Montreal, Canada. The school needed a new physics professor. J. J. Thomson wrote Ernest a recommendation, saying, "I have never had a student with more enthusiasm or ability for original research than Mr. Rutherford."

Ernest was sorry to leave Cambridge, but he knew the salary and title would bring his wedding day closer. He wrote to Mary, "Rejoice with me, my dear girl, for matrimony is looming in the distance."

Ernest was not as close as he had hoped, though. It was another year and a half before he had enough money to sail to New Zealand and bring Mary back with him. In the summer of 1900, Ernest and Mary were finally married.

Around the time Ernest arrived in Canada, John Cox, the head of the McGill physics department, said, "There seems to be nothing new going on in physics. The main things have all been found out and the work which remains is to carry on a great number of experiments and researches into relatively minor matters."

No one did a better job of proving John Cox wrong than Ernest.

At McGill, Ernest continued to study alpha and beta rays. These rays couldn't be seen, felt, heard, or touched. They could be detected only by observing their effect on other substances. No wonder they had gone unnoticed throughout history! And no wonder Ernest wanted to unveil their mystery.

In Canada, he was far away from the other scientists working on radioactivity. News about European developments took weeks to cross the Atlantic, but Ernest refused to be left out of the loop. He was so concerned about being left behind that he worked with incredible determination.

One of his first discoveries at McGill was a curious property of the radioactive element, thorium. Ernest noticed that as thorium gave off radioactive waves, it also emitted something else. He named the mysterious material an "emanation." Strangely, the emanation was also radioactive. In other words, it too, could produce alpha and beta rays.

Ernest had no idea what the emanation was, but he was determined to find out. He noticed that the radioactivity of this emanation diminished by half every 60 seconds. For example, after 1 minute, only one-half of the original radiation was left; after 2 minutes, only one-quarter remained; after 3 minutes, only one-eighth of the original radiation was left; and so on. Today, we know that every radioactive element has a *half-life*. The half-life is the amount of time the element takes to diminish in strength by one-half. Ernest was the first to notice it.

He began working with a young chemist named Frederick Soddy to figure out just what this mysterious thorium emanation was. For 2 years, the pair collaborated at McGill. Later, Fred described this time as the most hectic time of his life.

The emanation turned out to be some kind of invisible gas. Ernest and Fred named it thoron. But where did the thoron come from? It wasn't simply emitted from thorium like radioactive rays. Instead, something else in the thorium produced both the alpha rays and thoron. Ernest and Fred named this new substance thorium X.

Thus, the element thorium seemed to consist of three different substances—thorium, thorium X, and thoron. It is a testament to the creativity of the two men that they were able to understand the relationship between the three substances. They realized that as the element releases radioactive rays, it changes into an entirely different kind of atom. In other words, thorium atoms turn into thorium X atoms, and then thorium X atoms turn into thoron atoms.

This was a completely original idea. Previously, scientists were convinced that atoms couldn't change. They thought that an element always remained the same. Ernest and Fred showed that radioactive atoms could spontaneously turn into other atoms. It's as if thorium is the parent, thorium X is the daughter, and thoron is the grandchild. According to Ernest and Fred, other radioactive substances, such as radium and uranium, have similar "family trees."

If they were right, then alpha rays were probably emitted by the atom at the moment of transformation. In other words, when thorium released alpha rays, it became thorium X.

Unfortunately, other scientists were skeptical. Some members of McGill's faculty were worried that Ernest's wild ideas would embarrass the university. In a meeting of the McGill Physics Society, Ernest was warned to be more cautious. He became angry and began to defend his theory, speaking so quickly that no one could follow what he was saying. Luckily, John Cox rose to his defense. He predicted that history would regard Ernest's experimental work as monumental.

Even though Ernest was making major strides in the laboratory, he was still doing very badly as a teacher. He assumed that his students knew as much as he did. Finally, one class circulated a petition asking that Ernest not use calculus to teach physics. They explained that they couldn't follow his lectures because they had never taken a course in calculus.

Ernest was stunned. It had never occurred to him that his students might not understand calculus. Suddenly, he realized that he should pay more attention to what his students knew and didn't know. Slowly, his teaching methods began to improve.

During these years, Ernest's home life was good. Mary took care of the house and garden, and helped him organize his scientific work. She typed his papers, filed his lectures, and tried to straighten his lab. On March 30, 1901, their first child, Eileen Mary, was born.

ERNEST RUTHERFORD RETURNS TO ENGLAND

After 8 years in Canada, Ernest was ready to move back to England. In 1907, he became the head of the Physics Department at the University of Manchester.

Meanwhile, his teaching had improved a great deal. His students now considered him to be something of a showman. He created entire lectures around fantastic demonstrations. His assistant would set up and perform the experiments as Ernest dramatically raised

Ernest Rutherford is remembered as the father of nuclear science.

and lowered his voice to describe what the class was watching. His students received a sound education.

Although Ernest found teaching more fulfilling than he used to, his primary love was the laboratory— not the classroom. His personality dominated everything in his lab at Manchester. He was quick to criticize the students who worked with him when they fell behind, but he was also quick to encourage them when they did well. Many of the students that worked with Ernest went on to become world-famous scientists.

Age had not calmed Ernest's quick temper. If he was in a bad mood, he would stomp around, and everyone knew they should stay out of his way. When he was happy, Ernest would wander the halls bellowing "Onward Christian Soldiers" which wasn't much better since he was completely tone deaf.

Worst of all, Ernest's mood often changed from one moment to the next. When a student asked Ernest for money for new weights, Ernest exploded. He demanded to know why the student needed so much money. Couldn't he be more resourceful? Why couldn't he use containers of water, for example?

The student timidly replied that glass containers strong enough to hold so much water would cost more than the weights themselves. The student held his breath waiting for Ernest's reaction. To his relief, Ernest laughed, and walked away. A few moments later, Ernest was singing again.

Ernest's students worked on his favorite subject—alpha particles. Their first mission was to determine exactly what alpha particles are. They trapped several billion alpha particles in a glass chamber and examined them. They realized that alpha particles are just like helium atoms that have lost their electrons.

In 1908, after a year and a half at Manchester, Ernest was awarded the Nobel Prize for his work with radioactivity. Ernest was surprised to learn that he hadn't won a Nobel in physics, but in chemistry. At the ceremony in Stockholm, Rutherford said, "I have dealt with many different transformations with various periods of time, but the quickest I have ever seen is my own transformation in one moment from a physicist to a chemist."

Ernest's Nobel Prize was awarded for his work with radioactivity—not for discovering that inside each atom is a nucleus. He did not make the discovery for which he is best remembered until 1911.

Ernest was not particularly interested in developing a new model for the atom, or in deriving new theories. He liked to go into the lab, roll up his sleeves, and do experiments. He preferred figuring things out in the lab to figuring them out in his head.

Most of the time, he didn't accept theories developed by other scientists unless experiments proved them. There was one exception, however. Ernest trusted the atomic theory and model developed by one of the scientists who visited his laboratory—Niels Bohr.

During his 4 months at Manchester, Bohr practically lived in the lab. He spent his time developing a model of the hydrogen atom. According to his model, a hydrogen atom consists of one electron, which orbits a central nucleus—just as the moon orbits Earth. Heavier atoms have heavier nuclei and more electrons. Bohr thought that electrons could only move in very specific ways. He mapped out exactly what path the electrons would take as they circled the nucleus.

Scientists' view of the atom was changing very quickly. In just a few years, scientists had shown that an atom consists of electrons that are constantly moving around a central nucleus. This nucleus could change weight, transform an element from one substance to another, and send out a variety of mysterious rays. All these findings contributed to solving scientists' most basic question about atoms: What makes one element different from another? Soon, another student in Ernest's lab added another crucial piece to the puzzle.

Henry Gwyn-Jeffreys Moseley came to Manchester in 1910. His research showed that each element gives off a unique kind of X ray. By carefully studying these X rays, Moseley was able to determine how much positive charge was in the nucleus of various

*An artist's interpretation of the atomic model
proposed by Niels Bohr*

kinds of atoms. He noticed that the heavier an atom,
the greater its positive charge.

Moseley theorized that the nucleus of every atom
contains positively charged particles. These particles
weigh significantly more than electrons—2,000 times
more—so they account for most of an atom's weight.
Thus, Moseley reasoned, heavier elements contain a
greater number of these positively charged particles
than lighter elements. The number of negatively
charged electrons in each atom is equal to the number
of positively charged particles. This is why atoms have
no overall charge.

Scientists immediately embraced Moseley's idea. At first, most called these new particles "positive electrons." It was clear, however, that this name was not appropriate. In rejecting this name for the new particle, Rutherford once said, "I will not have an electron as big as a balloon in my laboratory." Eventually the positively charged particle was named a proton.

ERNEST RUTHERFORD'S RESEARCH DURING WORLD WAR I

On February 12, 1914, at Buckingham Palace, King George V knighted Ernest Rutherford for his service to the crown. He and Mary became Sir and Lady Rutherford. According to a letter Ernest wrote to a friend, Ernest's 13-year-old daughter had told her parents that she didn't think they were dignified enough for such a title.

Later that same year, World War I began. Rutherford helped the war effort with his scientific expertise. He worked to develop a system for tracking Germany's "silent submarines." These subs were a major threat because they could sneak up on ships and destroy them from below. Even though the engines of these submarines did make noise, it was difficult to distinguish that sound from other ocean noises. It was also hard to tell what direction the subs were coming from.

In one experiment, Ernest tried to figure out just what "notes" a submarine engine made. He worked with Sir Richard Paget, another prominent scientist, who happened to have perfect pitch. This means that whenever Sir Richard heard a noise, he could identify the corresponding note on the musical scale. Ernest and Richard went out on a small boat and arranged to have a submarine travel underneath them. As it passed by, Ernest held Richard by the heels while he immersed Richard's head and upper body in the water. Richard was supposed to identify the pitch of the submarine's engine.

While this experiment wasn't very successful, it did provide a humorous story that Ernest told with gusto for the rest of his life.

ERNEST RUTHERFORD RETURNS TO HIS FAVORITE RESEARCH

Whenever he had an opportunity, Ernest returned to his lab and performed experiments to better understand atoms. He found that when he aimed alpha particles at nitrogen atoms, the debris of the collision contained hydrogen atoms. Ernest could not explain this result. Where could the hydrogen come from? It was as if he had turned one kind of element into another. For centuries, alchemists and magicians had tried to turn common metals into gold. People had laughed at them, but no one was laughing now. Ernest seemed to have done it!

Before Ernest could figure out how nitrogen atoms formed hydrogen atoms, newspaper reporters somehow heard about his results. Article after article hailed Ernest as "the man who split the atom."

Ernest followed in J. J. Thomson's footsteps in other ways as well. World War I ended in November of 1918. Shortly thereafter, J. J. resigned from Cavendish Laboratory, and Ernest was invited to take over the job.

When Ernest arrived at Cavendish, there were about 600 physics students. Lecture rooms and labs were overcrowded. Some professors suggested that the lab reduce overcrowding by excluding female students. Ernest vigorously disagreed. Women had been attending the school since 1881, and he refused to take a step backward. In the end, women were allowed to stay, and Ernest did his best to add new laboratories and lecture rooms to his department instead.

While at Cavendish, Ernest continued to oversee work on the nucleus. It was during this time that he formally approved "proton" as the name for the positively charged particles in the nucleus.

It was also during Ernest's time at Cavendish that one of his students finally figured out what had happened in the experiment in which Ernest had split the atom. The student found that when an alpha particle and a nitrogen atom combined, they formed hydrogen as well as oxygen. The alpha particle, which is really just a helium nucleus, has two protons, while nitrogen has seven. Hydrogen has one proton, and oxygen has eight. In the collision, the helium had donated one of its protons to the nitrogen. The result was two entirely different elements. The total number of protons had remained the same, but they had moved from one atom to another. In other words, rearranging protons can result in completely different elements. This was an incredibly important discovery.

THE END OF ERNEST RUTHERFORD'S LIFE

Ernest's most important scientific work was done before he came to Cambridge. During his later years, Ernest spent a lot of time traveling around the world to give lectures about modern physics and the new model of the atom. He continued to win awards and was even given the title of Baron by the British monarchy. Ernest chose to be named Baron of Nelson, to honor his childhood home and the school where he was first introduced to physics.

By now, many other scientists had started studying the nucleus. They learned that atoms contain huge quantities of energy. Some visionaries even suggested that humans might be able to use this energy as fuel. As always, Ernest didn't believe fantastic ideas unless they were supported by experimental results.

In one lecture, he announced that, in his opinion, the idea that we'd ever be able to tap the energy trapped inside a nucleus was ridiculous. This lecture is memorable because he was so wrong. In both Europe and the United States, scientists were learning to do just that.

Ernest did not live to see the success of these experiments, however. On October 14, 1938, he fell ill from complications of a hernia. Doctors operated on him, but he failed to improve. He died 5 days later. He was cremated and his ashes were buried in Westminster Abbey near the graves of other great scientists, such as Lord Kelvin and Sir Isaac Newton. It was a fitting tribute to a man who had started a whole new branch of science.

A contemporary of Ernest's once said, "You're always at the crest of the wave." This statement was true. So was Ernest's reply, "Well, after all, I made the wave, didn't I?"

THREE

"THIS WILL DO IT"

Enrico Fermi and
the First Chain Reaction

On December 2, 1942, in the midst of World War II, a small group of scientists and government officials assembled on the balcony overlooking a squash court at the University of Chicago. Enrico Fermi stood in the middle of the court. Behind him, a pile of gray and black minerals stretched to the ceiling.

The minerals in the pile were the purest samples of graphite and uranium available. Layer upon layer had been laid down by carpenters, lab workers, and high school students over a 6-week period. The pile was so big that it contained more than enough graphite to make a pencil for every person in the world!

Enrico was about to reveal the results of his top-secret scientific experiments. He had found a way to capture energy from the nucleus of an atom. Four other scientists were on the court with Fermi. Three sat on top of the huge atomic pile. They were called the "suicide squad." If the demonstration did not go as

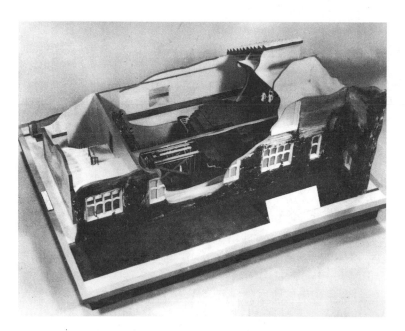

A scale model of the squash court where Enrico Fermi performed the experiment that created the first nuclear chain reaction.

planned, it was their job to flood the pile with cadmium. This would stop the experiment immediately.

The fourth physicist, George Weil, had the most important job. He controlled a cadmium rod that was stuck in the pile. As he slowly removed the rod, the uranium atoms in the pile would begin to split in two, or *fission*. Each time an atom split, energy as well as an extra neutron was released. This extra neutron would then collide into other atoms, causing them to split. This would release more energy and more neutrons. Just one or two free neutrons could start a *chain reaction*.

What is a chain reaction? Imagine what would happen if you spent hours, or even days, setting up an intricate pattern of dominoes. Just as it is possible to send hundreds of dominoes tumbling over with the flick of a finger, it is possible to create massive amounts of energy in a chain reaction that begins with just a couple of free bouncing neutrons.

Enrico explained to his audience that, as Weil pulled out the rod, the Geiger counters on the court would start measuring radioactivity. At the same time, other instruments would measure energy produced. The readings from these instruments would show the scientists and the observers that a chain reaction was occurring.

This was the first time Enrico had performed this experiment, so he was being very cautious. Even though his audience anxiously awaited the grand finale, Enrico refused to rush. He made the demostration last all day. He asked Weil to pull out the cadmium rod very slowly, inch by inch.

With each pull, the pile became more radioactive. Finally, at 3:20 P.M., Enrico said, "Pull it out another foot. This will do it. Now the pile will chain-react." The group watched the pile; nothing seemed to change. When they looked at the instruments, however, it was clear that a chain reaction had, indeed, begun. It was a monumental moment.

𝒴OUNG ENRICO FERMI

Enrico Fermi was born in Rome on September 29, 1901. He was the youngest of Alberto and Ida Fermi's three children. As a child, Enrico had few companions. He spent most of his time in secondhand bookstores, buying books on physics and math. Because the Fermis didn't have much money, they lived in a house without heating. When Enrico read, he tried to keep warm by sitting on his hands and turning the pages of his book with his tongue.

Young Enrico Fermi was so far ahead of the rest of his class that he studied on his own—teaching himself math, engineering, and physics. He taught himself well. When he applied to college in Pisa, his application stunned and impressed reviewers.

His entrance exam included complex mathematical techniques that many professors of the time would have had difficulty writing about. His scores stood out so much that one professor decided to give Enrico an oral exam. The professor didn't think that a high-school student could possibly know so much. At the end of the interview, the professor announced that he had never seen such a gifted student.

Enrico went to college at a time when some of the greatest revolutions in physics were occurring. The nucleus had been discovered a decade earlier. Niels Bohr and other physicists were hammering out the details of how electrons move. Albert Einstein had recently proposed his theories of relativity.

Enrico knew about all these findings, but not because he learned them in his classes. He read about them in scientific papers published by researchers as they made new discoveries. Most of Enrico's professors didn't understand the complex concepts presented in these papers. In fact, one professor, Luigi Puccianti, asked Enrico for lessons in modern physics.

Enrico's special relationship with Puccianti worked to his benefit, especially when Enrico became involved with the Anti-Neighbors Society, a group that often played pranks on other students. On one occasion, the group went too far and released a stink bomb in the middle of a lecture. Enrico would have been expelled if Professor Puccianti had not urged the university to let him stay.

In July of 1922, at the age of 20, Enrico graduated magna cum laude with a Ph.D. in physics. He returned to Rome, where he met a well-respected Italian physicist, Orso Mario Corbino. Orso Corbino had a dream. He wanted Italy to improve its international reputation in physics. He thought Enrico could help him.

Corbino helped Enrico get a job as a physics professor at the University of Rome. With all the changes in science, some of the older people in the department refused to believe the new theories. Enrico quickly became friends with a group of professors and students who were dedicated to bringing modern physics to Rome.

This group jokingly gave themselves titles based on those used by the Roman Catholic Church. Enrico was nicknamed the Pope; other members were referred to as Cardinals, Vicars, and Inquisitors.

One summer, Fermi announced to his friends that he felt like doing something out of the ordinary. He decided that he would either buy a car or take a wife. Of course, they all knew Enrico was thinking of proposing to Laura Capon, an engineering student with whom he had become close friends. Laura heard about Enrico's bold statement. When he drove up in a brand-new yellow Peugeot, she was profoundly disappointed.

"All was not lost, however," Laura wrote many years later in her biography of Enrico. "Fermi was to indulge in greater extravagance than planned. He had bought a car and, within a few months, he took a wife as well. Thus, I came to share ownership of the Peugeot." Laura and Enrico Fermi were married on July 19, 1928.

Enrico Fermi with this wife, Laura, and their children

The scientific community of the late 1920s was just beginning to understand what was inside the nucleus. It was becoming common knowledge that the nucleus contains protons, and that the number of protons in the nucleus determines the type of atom. For example, hydrogen has one proton, helium has two, and lithium has three.

In 1932, James Chadwick discovered the neutron. Ernest Rutherford had predicted that such a particle must exist because it was the only way to fully explain atomic weight. If there were only protons in a nucleus, helium would be twice as heavy as hydrogen, and lithium would be three times heavier then hydrogen. In reality, helium is four times heavier than hydrogen and lithium is six times heavier. There

could be only one explanation for the extra weight—
there must be some other mysterious particle inside
the nucleus.

$\mathcal{U}$NDERSTANDING NEUTRONS

Although Ernest Rutherford predicted that neutrons
exist and James Chadwick found and described them,
Enrico Fermi was one of the first people to really understand how they behave and how they can be ma-
nipulated. Enrico also figured out the relationship
between neutrons and a kind of radioactivity called
beta rays. A beta ray is really an electron, but it does
not move around the nucleus as normal electrons do.
Instead, it is released from inside the nucleus.

Enrico discovered that, in a radioactive nucleus, a
neutron sometimes transforms into an electron and a
proton. When this happens, the proton remains, but the
electron is immediately hurled out of the atom as a beta
ray. Since the number of protons in the nucleus determines whether an atom is, say, uranium or thorium or
lead, the presence of an extra proton in the nucleus
changes the atom from one kind of element to another.

Enrico suspected that there was an unknown
force that caused the neutron to disintegrate. He
named it the *weak force.* At the time, scientists believed that there are only two forces in the universe—
gravity and electromagnetism. When Enrico tried to
publish a paper describing the weak force, he was
strongly criticized. The editors of the journal refused
to publish his paper. Today, physicists around the
world realize that Enrico was right. In fact, one of the
numbers used to calculate the weak force is called the
Fermi constant.

While Enrico was hard at work in Rome, Irène Curie, the daughter of Marie and Pierre, and her husband Frédéric Joliot were investigating artificial radioactivity in Paris. Working together, the couple discovered how to make phosphorus, a stable element, radioactive.

To do this, Irène and Frédéric aimed alpha rays at aluminum. An alpha particle has two protons. When the rays hit the nucleus of an aluminum atom, these protons were incorporated into the nucleus. As a result, the aluminum transformed into a radioactive form of phosphorus. If you look at the periodic table of elements, you can see that phosphorus (P) has two more protons than aluminum (Al).

Irène Curie with her husband and research partner, Frédéric Joliot

Irène and Frédéric's discovery caught Enrico Fermi's attention. He decided to try to make other elements radioactive. He did not want to use the same method as Irène and Frédéric, however. He thought that shooting positively charged alpha particles into a positively charged nucleus would be like trying to force the wrong sides of two magnets together—they would naturally repel each other. Instead, Enrico used neutrons. Neutrons have no charge and Enrico suspected that they would slip right into the nucleus.

He set up his equipment, and got to work. One by one, he shot neutrons into each of the elements. First he tried hydrogen, then lithium, then beryllium, and so on. He followed the same order as the periodic table of elements.

At first, he found nothing. But when he bombarded element number nine—fluorine—with neutrons, it became radioactive. Soon, he had made radioactive forms of many elements. Just 2 months after Irène and Frédéric's announcement, Enrico published a paper explaining that neutrons are a much better tool for creating artificial radioactivity.

Soon after this, Enrico figured out a way to make radioactive elements in a more efficient way. He and his colleagues put a block of wax between the source of the neutrons and a sample of silver. Before reaching the silver, the neutrons had to pass through the wax. At the end of the experiment, the silver was about 100 times more radioactive than a sample that had been bombarded with neutrons before the wax block was put in place.

The scientists were amazed by their results. None understood why the wax made the sample so much more radioactive. Enrico tried to work out a possible explanation in his mind. He knew that wax contains a lot of hydrogen. When the neutrons passed through the wax, he reasoned, they must have bounced off the nuclei of the hydrogen atoms. Apparently, the nuclei acted like speed bumps—they forced the neutrons to slow down. Slower neutrons had a better chance of hitting a nucleus.

Enrico wanted to test his idea immediately. If he was right, then water, which also has lots of hydrogen, should have the same effect as wax. He and a small group of other Italian physicists moved their equipment to the banks of a goldfish pond in Orso Corbino's garden. They placed a silver sample in the water and shot neutrons toward it. At the end of the experiment, the silver was just as radioactive as the sample used in the wax-barrier experiment. Enrico was right. The physicists were ecstatic!

The scientists rushed over to one of their student's homes to write up a paper that would announce their discovery to the whole world. They were so enthusiastic that when they finally left, a maid asked if all the guests had been drunk.

ROAD TO THE FIRST CHAIN REACTION

In 1933, Adolf Hitler became the leader of Germany. Next, he set his sights on conquering the rest of Europe. In 1936, his army invaded France. Two years later, he seized control of Austria. In 1939, Hitler's troops invaded Poland, and World War II began. In 1940, the Nazis conquered, Denmark, Norway, the Netherlands, Belgium, Luxembourg, and France. A few months later, Benito Mussolini, the dictator of Italy, officially declared war on France and Great Britain.

*Adolf Hitler and his Nazi Army conquered much
of Europe in the early days of World War II.*

Meanwhile, Hitler had started a campaign against
the Jews. New laws were written that restricted Jewish
rights. Thousands left the country as quickly as they
could. Thousands more were less fortunate; they were
sent to concentration camps. Similar laws were passed
in Italy. The Italian government seized the passports
of all Jewish citizens, making it impossible for them to
leave the country.

For most of his life, Enrico Fermi had ignored politics, but these new laws affected him directly because
his wife was Jewish. Enrico quickly realized that Italy
was no longer a safe place for his family.

On November 10, 1938, Enrico received a phone
call from Stockholm, Sweden. He had won the Nobel

Prize for his work with slow neutrons and artificial radioactivity. Surely the Italian government would allow the Fermis to travel to Stockholm, so that Enrico could accept his prestigious award. The Fermis decided that this was their chance to escape.

They packed small bags to make it seem as though they were leaving Italy for only a few days. After accepting the Nobel Prize, Enrico and his family boarded a ship and sailed to the United States. The Fermis had been forced to leave behind almost all their possessions, but they were alive and they were together.

On January 2, 1939, the Fermis landed in New York. While Laura and Enrico struggled to learn English, their children picked up American slang very quickly. One day, when Laura told her 4-year-old son to wash his hands, he responded, "You can't make me, this is a free country." Every American child has made a similar statement at one time or another, but, to the Fermis, it was completely new. Enrico liked it so much that soon he was using the same phrase.

A few months later, Enrico learned that one of the experiments he had done while he was in Italy was not as simple as it had seemed. Soon after discovering how to slow neutrons, Enrico had aimed them at samples of uranium—the heaviest atom known at the time. He thought the neutrons were absorbed by the nuclei, making an atom even heavier than uranium. Enrico believed that he had created a brand-new element.

Enrico was wrong. Additional research showed that when neutrons slammed into the nuclei of uranium, something unexpected happened—the uranium split it into two smaller atoms—each was about half the size of uranium. This was the process of fission, which Enrico would later turn into a chain reaction.

Enrico quickly realized that there was something very interesting about splitting uranium by bombarding it with neutrons. The original uranium atom was heavier than the combined weights of the two resulting atoms. The missing material had turned into pure energy.

Even this might not have been such an important discovery, except that each collision also released an additional neutron. This neutron could collide with another uranium atom and force it to fission. As long as plenty of pure uranium was available, it was only a matter of time before a chain reaction occurred.

Scientists understood the importance of this type of reaction immediately. If they could learn to control the process, they could produce a whole new kind of power plant to produce electricity. Because the plant would not have to burn materials to produce energy, this type of energy would reduce air and water pollution.

The scientists also realized that sustained fission could be used to power the most destructive bombs ever seen. This idea caught the attention of the United States government. Even though large-scale fission was still nothing more than a theory, the United States wanted to make sure that they tested its possibilities before the Germans did. Enrico Fermi was the obvious person to work on the project. After all, he knew more about neutrons than anyone else.

For a chain reaction to continue, each neutron released by one atom had to hit the nucleus of another atom. And, in order for this to happen, the neutrons had to be moving very slowly. To understand why, imagine a game of miniature golf. If your golf ball is not too far from the hole, it is better to hit the ball gently. If you hit the ball too hard, it will probably shoot right past the hole. A slower golf ball will fall into the hole.

Neutrons are similar to golf balls. If they are moving slowly, they are more likely to hit a nucleus. Nobody was better at creating slow neutrons than Enrico Fermi.

In 1942, the United States government decided to concentrate all war research in Chicago. In April, the Fermis set up their home there, and Enrico went to work at the University of Chicago's Metallurgical Laboratory.

Enrico's first task was to find the best way to slow the neutrons released by fissioning atoms. He knew that water was one possibility, but he found that it absorbed many of the neutrons in the process. This meant that they were not available to hit the nuclei of other uranium atoms. Every neutron was precious.

Enrico decided to try graphite. Since graphite—like water—contains a lot of hydrogen atoms, Enrico theorized that very pure graphite would slow down neutrons without absorbing them. If he had a very large pile of graphite, he would be able to initiate a chain reaction. Enrico wanted to test his idea, but he knew careful planning was very important. He had access to only a few tons of uranium, so there was no room for error. He had to get it right the first time.

Enrico's care and patience paid off. His squash-court demonstration proved to the world that it was possible to create a chain reaction. A chain reaction with slow neutrons meant a new source of energy for heat and electricity. If a slow-neutron chain reaction could be induced, then perhaps a fast-neutron chain reaction was also possible. If so, the United States could build a bomb that would help them win World War II.

To celebrate the occasion, physicist Eugene Wigner broke out a bottle of Chianti wine. Afterward, the five scientists who had conducted the experiment signed the bottle. One of them, Al Wattenberg, took the bottle home and kept it as a souvenir.

Ten years later, Wattenberg mailed the bottle to a tenth-anniversary celebration at the University of Chicago. He insured the bottle for $1,000, which aroused the curiosity of the media and led to dozens of newspaper articles. A few months later, Enrico and the other physicists each received a free case of Chianti from an importer who was grateful for all the free advertising.

THE NEXT STEP

Now that Enrico had shown that a slow chain reaction was possible, the time had come to build a fast one. The Fermis moved to a top secret government lab called Los Alamos in New Mexico. Many scientists were doing war research there. Enrico was put in charge of the F Division, which stood for Fermi, or rather, Farmer. Since everyone at Los Alamos was given a fake name, Enrico was known as Eugene Farmer.

On July 16, 1945, Fermi was involved in another monumental test. That morning he and a group of other scientists set up an experimental bomb in the Alamagordo Desert near Los Alamos. When the bomb exploded, the physicists watched from 10 miles

The world's first atomic bomb, called the
Trinity device, was detonated on July 16, 1945.

(16 km) away. They saw a blinding flash of light and heard a great thunderous roar.

Enrico was the only one who did not look on as the bomb exploded. He was too absorbed in another experiment. At the moment of the explosion, Enrico threw a bunch of confetti up in the air. The aftershock from the bomb carried the pieces of paper through the air. By measuring how far the confetti traveled, Enrico was able to determine the force of the blast. The army had equipment to measure the blast too, but Enrico's simple method allowed him to get an answer long before the army did.

On August 6, 1945, the United States dropped an atomic bomb on Hiroshima, Japan. On August 9, they dropped a second bomb on Nagasaki, Japan. On August 14, Japan surrendered, ending World War II.

Even today, some people wonder whether the United States should have used this incredible weapon, or even whether it should have been built. According to Laura, Enrico believed that it would have been useless to stop the research. According to him, nothing is served by trying to halt the progress of science.

Enrico Fermi produced the first self-sustaining nuclear chain reaction.

*The world's first atomic bomb just before it was
tested in the Alamagordo Desert*

THE MEN BEHIND THE BOMB

Robert Oppenheimer witnessed this momentous
event firsthand. He had led the scientists during those
years at Los Alamos. Robert had loved New Mexico
since he was a child. He once said, "I have two loves,
physics and the desert. It pains me that I can see no
way to bring them together."

Not long after making this statement, Robert was
able to fulfill his dream. It had been his idea to set up
the top-secret physics lab in the middle of New Mexico. In the end, the project didn't make him as happy
as he'd hoped. As that first bomb exploded, a line
from Hindu mythology floated through Robert's
head, "I have become death, shatterer of worlds."

*Robert Oppenheimer
(left) and General
Leslie Groves (right)
just before the first
nuclear bomb test*

Robert had spent most of his early life preoccupied with his thoughts and ideas. He was the stereotypical absent-minded professor—a brilliant man whose brain was filled with so much science, math, and philosophy that there wasn't much room for what was going on in day-to-day life. All that changed when he became the head of the United States bomb research, called the Manhattan Project. He suddenly became involved with one of the century's greatest controversies. The bombs he helped build were dropped on

Japan, killing hundreds of thousands of people. He always felt responsible for what he had created.

Ernest Orlando Lawrence wasn't at the site the day of the explosion, but he had been part of the project, too. Unlike Robert, everyone had known Ernest's name long before the war. Ernest was talkative and friendly, and the media liked to write about him. As one of the country's most famous scientists, it was natural that he was part of the Manhattan Project, too.

Ernest was well known because he had invented the cyclotron, a machine that could smash open a nucleus. At the time, his cyclotron was the biggest and most expensive piece of physics equipment ever invented. A cyclotron whirled protons round and round in a circle until they were moving so fast that a proton split open the nucleus of the atom when the two collided. The cyclotron was the precursor of the atom-smashers or *particle accelerators* that physicists use today.

Before the cyclotron was built, scientists did their experiments with little money and whatever equipment happened to be lying around the lab. Ernest changed all that. He had an entirely different vision of how to do science. He had a dominating personality, and he wanted to do big experiments.

Ernest was not discouraged when other scientists told him that the machines he wanted to build would never work or were too expensive. He just plowed ahead, always making sure he got his way. It was this single-mindedness that helped him build the cyclotron when no other scientist thought it possible.

These two men, one who opened the nucleus and one who harnessed its energy, helped bring science into the public eye. They began as friends and ended as enemies.

Ernest Lawrence

*Y*OUNG ERNEST LAWRENCE

Ernest Orlando Lawrence grew up in a small town in South Dakota. As a student at the University of South Dakota, he discovered that he had a talent for physics. His natural ability was obvious to his teachers, too. At one lecture, Ernest's professor made an announcement: "Class, this is Ernest Lawrence. Take a good look at him, for there will come a day when you'll be proud to have been in the same class with him."

What made Ernest such a good student? He had an intuitive understanding of electronics and magnetism that allowed him to do experiments that others found difficult. He never spent too much time working out the math or the equations behind an experiment. He just couldn't wait to get his hands on the equipment.

Ernest had a mentor named Professor Swann who encouraged him, saying, "Sometimes a scientist needs to work out all the theory down to the very last bit of math, but other times the most efficient way to get the job done is to sit in the laboratory and do the experiment over and over until you make it work."

Because Ernest relied on his lab experience more than anything else, he did not always do well on basic physics exams. However, his prowess in the lab was undeniable. He earned a Ph.D. in June of 1925 when he was 26 years old.

Soon, he became an assistant professor at Yale. Yale was one of the most prestigious places to be a scientist in the 1920s, but Ernest wasn't happy there. He was ambitious and wanted to become famous. He didn't think Yale gave him enough money or power to succeed. Ernest believed that if he didn't make a major discovery by the time he was 30 years old, he never would.

So Ernest did something very daring. He left Yale and went to a state school that wasn't nearly as well known. He became a professor at the University of California, Berkeley. Ernest made the right choice. Berkeley's reputation and prestige grew tremendously over the years, and Ernest worked there for the rest of his life.

𝒴OUNG ROBERT OPPENHEIMER

As much as Ernest Lawrence was a country boy, J. Robert Oppenheimer was not. Robert was born in New York City on April 22, 1904, to Julius and Ella

Oppenheimer. Because his family was affluent, he grew up with servants who drove him everywhere, cleaned up after him, and kept him sheltered from the outside world. His family expected him to go to the very best schools, so it was no surprise that he went to Harvard.

Robert was a chemistry major, but he always dabbled in other things, too. Poetry, painting, and philosophy were among his other interests. In fact, he had so many interests that he didn't know which profession to choose until his last year at Harvard. That's when he took a physics course—and loved it. When he graduated from Harvard in 1925, he promptly set sail for graduate school at Cavendish Laboratory at Cambridge University in England.

Robert Oppenheimer was not like Ernest in the lab either. He hated being a research physicist. He wasn't good at it. What Robert did like about physics was the theories. But coming up with new theories wasn't always easy for Robert. He would stand alone in front of a blackboard holding a piece of chalk, waiting for inspiration to strike. He would mumble to himself, "the point is . . . the point is . . . the point is . . ." Hours would pass before he figured out what the point was. Robert was 22 years old, depressed, and worried that he would never succeed in science.

Eventually, he decided he was better suited for a school that focused more on physics theory than on research and experiments. He transferred to the University of Göttingen in Germany—another of the great physics universities in Europe. Suddenly, things started looking up. He said later, "I felt completely relieved of the responsibility to go back into a lab. I hadn't been good, I hadn't done anybody any good, and I hadn't had any fun whatsoever."

Unfortunately, the other students at Göttingen didn't respond well to Robert. He often interrupted people—students and professors—to point out their mistakes. Most of the students thought he was just showing off. Robert didn't realize that he was treating people badly. He was completely unaware of the world around him. In fact, he was so out of touch with day-to-day requirements that he never officially registered as a student. Although the school was annoyed, they did award him a Ph.D.

In 1929, Robert was offered a part-time position at Berkeley. That is where he and Ernest finally met.

BUILDING THE WORLD'S FIRST CYCLOTRON

At the time, Ernest was interested in developing a new way to study the nucleus. He once said, "The nucleus is like a fly inside a cathedral." Ernest wanted to smash open the cathedral to study every part of that fly. He thought he could do it by using speeding protons—or more specifically hydrogen *ions*—to crack the nucleus open. An ion is an atom that has either lost or gained an electron. As a result, it is no longer electrically neutral. Since a hydrogen atom has only one electron, when that electron is removed, it is essentially the same as a free-floating proton.

The trick was to get the ions moving fast enough. Work done by other scientists had shown that the best way to control protons was with an electric field. Ernest knew that if he could devise a scheme to speed up those protons faster than anyone had done before, he'd be able to open up the nucleus.

In early 1929, Ernest came across an article by Rolf Wideroe that included a diagram showing a long tube that could energize a proton with 25,000 volts. This alone would not have impressed Ernest, but Rolf Wideroe had done something clever. He had placed a second tube at the end of the first one. The second tube delivered the same electric kick as the first tube. As a result, the protons moved even faster.

Ernest had a revelation. Perhaps he could energize and control protons with successive kicks of a small amount of energy instead of needing an impossibly large amount of electricity. There was only one problem—it would take an incredibly long tube to get the ion up to the right speed. Then he had a second revelation. What if the tube went round and round in a circle? Magnets could be used to keep the hydrogen ions moving. But those kicks of energy would still have to come at just the right moment.

Imagine pushing a swing. If you push it when it's at its lowest point, the swing will actually slow down. If you want the swing to reach its maximum height and speed, you must push it at just the right moment. Protons moving in an accelerator are similar to a swing. If you want them to reach their maximum speed, you must zap them with electricity at just the right moment.

This might seem impossible. After all, how could Ernest time the energy correctly for all the protons? At first, Ernest thought of the protons as runners on a track. At any given moment, different protons would be in different parts of the tube.

Ernest quickly scribbled down some math. His calculations showed him something remarkable. It turns out that protons moving in a magnetic field *always* take the same amount of time to travel around a circular tube—no matter how big the circle. If the circle is small, the protons go slower. If the circle is larger, the protons go faster. This means that all the protons will be ready for the next kick of energy at the same time.

Ernest easily figured out how to give the protons a series of small, perfectly timed jolts of energy until they reached the speed required to smash open a nucleus. Within minutes, Ernest had a plan. For the next few weeks, Ernest talked to people about his proton-smasher until their eyes glazed over. He discussed his idea with Robert Oppenheimer while they took long walks together. Ernest was sure that his cyclotron would work.

Most people admired Ernest's enthusiasm, but thought his idea was ridiculous. Luckily, Ernest trusted his own intuition more than he trusted the opinions of other scientists. "The history of science is full of examples of theory being wrong," he said to colleagues.

Ernest devoted all his time and energy to building the world's first cyclotron. He was a phenomenal director. He developed a plan and assigned a specific task to each of the graduate students working for him. He didn't spend much time hacking out the nuts and bolts. He let his students work out the practical details of how to carry out his ideas.

He demanded that they work well into the night, abandoning their own social lives. Some of the more clever students learned how to get around this. When they needed to go out, they would leave their coat and hat in the lab. That way if Ernest came by unexpectedly, he would assume they were in a another part of the building.

All the hard work paid off. When Ernest was 29 years old, he presented a lecture about his machine at a meeting of the National Academy of Sciences. Every scientist in the room listened attentively. They were intrigued by the little device—a small circular glass box surrounded by a magnetic field—on the table next to Ernest. He told the group that when he turned his device on, it sent the protons inside around and around in circles. He concluded his presentation by saying that a larger version of this device would be capable of zapping protons with a million volts of electricity. This would provide the protons with enough energy to smash open a nucleus.

The New York Times heard about Ernest's incredible accomplishments. The newspaper ran an article about his research the next day. Soon, "Ernest Lawrence" was a household name. Ernest had accomplished his goal—he had made a major contribution to science before turning 30 years old.

As it turns out, Ernest's little box wasn't as impressive as he claimed. This first box didn't work! Stanley Livingston, one of Ernest's students, built the first working cyclotron. To do this, Stanley made two semicircular brass boxes. A magnet in each box kept the protons moving in a circle. When the protons crossed the gap between the boxes, they would be exposed to an electric field and speed up. Each zap delivered 2,000 volts to the protons. As the protons whizzed around the circular track, they could be energized with a total of 80,000 volts. Ernest was very excited; this first cyclotron worked just as he had imagined.

Next, Ernest wanted to build an even bigger cyclotron—one that could deliver a total of 1 million volts to the protons inside. To build this cyclotron, Ernest would need a lot more money. Luckily, he could inspire investors as well as students.

Over the next few months, Ernest became a first -class fund-raiser. At a time when most physicists were working on shoestring budgets, Ernest managed to

*Stanley Livingston (left) and Ernest O. Lawrence (right)
pose in front an early atom smasher.*

raise almost $10,000. Ernest's cyclotrons grew larger and larger. Eventually, he outgrew the Berkeley Physics Department. His equipment was moved to a new building, and a new department was created. What began as Ernest's space is now known as the Lawrence Berkeley Lab, one of the most prestigious research centers in the world.

In February of 1932, the million-volt cyclotron became a reality. Unfortunately, Ernest had been so focused on building the cyclotron that he lost sight of his original goal. Two British scientists were the first to crack open a nucleus. It turns out that protons don't really need as much energy as Ernest had imagined to open up a nucleus.

Ernest heard about what the two scientists had accomplished while he was on his honeymoon with Mary Blumer. He sent a telegram back to his lab: "Get lithium from chemistry department and start preparations to repeat with the cyclotron. Will be back shortly."

When Ernest's team repeated the experiment, they got even more spectacular results than the British lab. In the end, Ernest Lawrence was not the first scientist to break open a nucleus, but the cyclotron certainly lived up to his expectations. It was the perfect new technique for studying the atom.

ROBERT OPPENHEIMER GETS INVOLVED

While Ernest was dazzling the world, Robert Oppenheimer was quietly working on the theories behind the movement of atoms. Although Robert did not become a public figure while he was at Berkeley, he was very popular with his students. They adored him, and many tried to emulate him. A few even tried to copy his stiff walk.

Not everyone got along with Robert, though. He was always sharp-tongued. He hadn't learned from his experiences at the University of Göttingen. He still interrupted both professors and students, and he seemed to take pleasure in pointing out other people's mistakes. Robert was so wrapped up in his own thoughts that he didn't realize how people were reacting to him. There would always be people who resented Robert.

Initially, Robert also had trouble staying in touch

with what was going on around him. The stock market had crashed in 1929, setting off the Great Depression. But Robert didn't find out about it until 1930. It was Ernest who told him.

Robert had never been exposed to poverty. He had never realized that millions of people were struggling just to get enough to eat. Suddenly Robert's whole outlook changed. He began to pay more attention to politics, and he joined groups that helped the poor and oppressed. Like many other scholars, he had some contact with the Communist Party. Although he never became a member, he did participate in some of their efforts to help the poor and defend human rights.

When World War II started in Europe, Robert was very concerned. Germany was invading other countries and trying to exterminate the Jewish people. Robert wanted to do what he could to stop Hitler.

Like many other scientists, he realized that if all the energy stored in the nuclei of a uranium sample could be released at the same time, a huge explosion would occur. Although Robert had never been particularly interested in nuclear science, he felt obliged to help protect the world from Hitler.

He began to think about how a nuclear bomb might be built. Soon, he became a consultant to a group of scientists working in the Metallurgical Laboratory at the University of Chicago. He helped them develop a plan that outlined how a fission bomb might work.

According to the plan, the bomb would consist of a spherically shaped sample of uranium with a hollow cylinder running through it. Free neutrons in the uranium would occasionally hit a uranium nucleus and force it to fission. If the sample of uranium was large and dense enough, there might be enough free neutrons to create a chain reaction. If most of the uranium atoms fissioned simultaneously, a powerful explosion would occur.

For a chain reaction to begin, a uranium sample must be a specific size. The weight of the uranium sphere would be a little smaller than that critical size. To set off the bomb, more uranium would be shot into an empty cylinder in the center of the uranium ball. That additional uranium would make the total sample just big enough for a chain reaction to occur. Within milliseconds, an explosion would light up the sky.

Robert was invited to join the team of scientists working at the University of Chicago. For years, Robert's peers had thought of him as absent-minded and socially awkward, but now, in a very short time, Robert had made a complete transformation.

He realized that, when he put his mind to it, he had a gift for organizing. In fact, he was a natural leader. He could conduct meetings and presentations with ease. Whenever he was at the podium, he encouraged everyone to speak out. He helped the other scientists frame their ideas, and kept the discussion on the right track.

THE DISCOVERY OF PLUTONIUM

Meanwhile, Ernest wasn't thinking about the war at all. He was still smashing open nuclei in his atom smasher. Nevertheless, he stumbled on a discovery that eventually made all the difference in the world to the team working on the bomb.

One of Ernest's students tested a uranium sample

in the cyclotron. He bombarded it with protons to see if he could get it to fission. The uranium split in two, just as the scientists had expected. But the experiment had also produced something they had not anticipated—faint smudges. When Edward MacMillan (one of Ernest's students) examined the smudges, he realized that they were traces of an unknown element. Scientists had discovered many new elements in the past few decades, but there was something different about this one—it was heavier than uranium.

For years, scientists had believed that uranium was the heaviest element. Ever since the days of Ernest Rutherford, scientists had accepted that a heavier element could not exist. This new element, which MacMillan named neptunium, had ninety-three protons. The neptunium wasn't very stable, and it quickly transformed. Amazingly, the result of the transformation was another new element with ninety-four protons. MacMillan named this element plutonium.

As scientists spent more time studying these new elements, they realized that inducing a chain reaction with plutonium would be much easier than creating a chain reaction with uranium. Plutonium was a better material for making a nuclear bomb.

In 1939, Ernest was awarded the Nobel Prize. His invention, the cyclotron, had revolutionized the way scientists studied the atom. Because World War II was in full swing, Ernest didn't want to travel to Stockholm to accept the award. Instead, the Swedish general consul delivered the prize to him.

A few months after Ernest received this prestigious prize, Robert had a celebration of his own. He married Kitty Puening, a young woman who had just earned a biology degree from the University of Pennsylvania. Like Robert, Kitty was politically active. In fact, at one point, she had been a member of the Communist Party.

THE EFFORT CONTINUES AT LOS ALAMOS

When the Japanese bombed Pearl Harbor and the United States entered World War II, the government became even more interested in the effort to build a nuclear bomb. General Leslie Groves was assigned to oversee the project. He wasn't happy about his new assignment. He had never worked with scientists before, and he didn't really understand the physical prin-

The Japanese attack on Pearl Harbor brought the United States into World War II.

ciples underlying fission. He became angry when no seemed to be able to explain it to him. "The scientists had lots of theories," he said later, "but they didn't know anything." He was very frustrated.

When Groves arrived at Berkeley, Ernest Lawrence invited him to the lab and made him feel comfortable. Robert Oppenheimer sat down with Groves and carefully explained the theories behind fission and told him how they planned to build a nuclear bomb. Groves had finally found two scientists he liked.

More and more, Groves turned to Robert for advice. Robert believed that the only way to get the project done right was to move a group of scientists to a secret location where they could devote all their time to it. He thought a secluded spot in the desert might work well. The two men picked a boys' school on the top of a hill called Los Alamos. The site was about an hour's drive from Santa Fe, New Mexico.

At first Oppenheimer thought that about 30 scientists would be working in the lab with him. By the end of the project, however, there were more than 300 scientists at Los Alamos. The little school on the hill had been transformed into a small town.

The research that took place at the Los Alamos lab was the beginning of what scientists now refer to as "big science." In the past, scientists generally worked in separate labs on separate projects. They worked at their own pace and were driven by nothing more than their own curiosity. Scientists worked on tight budgets and periodically had to apply to their university or outside organizations for funding.

But the effort to build the bomb—the Manhattan Project—was quite different. In a way, Ernest's effort to build the cyclotron had been a stepping stone. That project had required a great deal of money, but no one could deny its success. The cyclotron had brought physics to a whole new level.

The Manhattan Project went much further than the cyclotron project. The United States government gave the lab all the money it needed and, in return, demanded that the scientists work around the clock.

It was an exciting time. Never had so many great scientists been gathered together to achieve a common goal. The scientists were driven. They knew that building this bomb might be the only way to win the war, the only way to stop Germany and Japan, the only way to preserve democracy. In addition, many of the scientists were Jews. They were horrified by what Hitler was doing to their relatives in Europe.

One group figured out how to ignite the bomb; another studied how the nucleus fissions; and yet another built the casing for the bomb. Many of the scientists were so focused on their individual projects that they didn't see the big picture. It was easy for them to forget that, ultimately, they were creating a weapon of mass destruction.

Through it all, Robert Oppenheimer led the effort at Los Alamos with flair. He encouraged everyone to pursue whatever ideas they had. Most of the scientists considered him helpful and considerate. When they went to him with an idea, he grasped the theory behind it quickly and urged them to keep up the good work.

Not everyone thought of Robert as an effective leader, however. Instead of seeing him as charming and brilliant, they considered him calculating and manipulative.

One scientist that Robert rubbed the wrong way was Edward Teller. Robert did not encourage Teller as much as he supported some other scientists. He knew that Teller had good ideas, but they were too complex. (As it turned out, Teller's ideas laid the groundwork for the next generation of nuclear bombs.) Edward resented Robert for not paying more attention to his ideas. Teller also disliked Robert's habit of interrupting people to point out their mistakes. As time passed, his dislike for Robert grew and grew.

Ernest began to have problems with Robert, too. Before the war started, Ernest had set out to build the biggest cyclotron yet. He had raised enough money to build a 100-million-volt cyclotron, but Robert and other scientists didn't think it could be done.

In order for protons to be energized with 100 million volts of electricity, they would have to be moving close to the speed of light. Albert Einstein had shown that nothing in the universe could travel faster than the speed of light. In addition, it was very difficult to get matter to travel even close to this speed.

Robert couldn't convince Ernest that the 100-million-volt cyclotron was a lost cause. As usual, Ernest didn't listen to what other people said. But the two scientists had such different ideas about science that they stopped discussing physics with each other. This, of course, put a tremendous strain on their friendship.

Ernest's huge cyclotron was never finished. Although Ernest didn't work at Los Alamos, he never lost sight of the importance of the Manhattan Project. He knew that the scientists at Los Alamos needed a supply of pure uranium, so he took his new cyclotron apart and used the parts to build a machine that would purify uranium. His new particle accelerator was called the calutron (for *cali*fornia *u*niversity). It produced enough uranium for research, but not enough for a bomb.

As it turned out, no one could produce enough pure uranium for what the government had in mind. Several labs around the country had spent a great deal of time purifying uranium. After years of work, there was only enough uranium to build one bomb. One bomb was not enough to win the war.

This was bad news for the scientists at Los Alamos. They had not anticipated this problem. They had tried to develop both a uranium bomb and a plutonium bomb, but so far only the design for the uranium bomb seemed promising. The scientists scrambled for a solution to their dilemma.

Robert's design wouldn't work with plutonium. Plutonium fissions so easily that attempting to build a plutonium sphere would be useless. The ball would begin to disintegrate before it was large enough to explode.

It took more than a year to develop a design that worked. The scientists began with a large sphere of plutonium that wasn't dense enough to fission spontaneously. Next, they forced the plutonium sample into a smaller space. Whenever a material is forced into a smaller space, its density increases. If this procedure was done perfectly, a chain reaction would begin. Within moments, the plutonium would explode.

Plutonium is not a liquid or a gas. Instead, it is a solid material—as hard as rock. As a result, it is not easy to force it into a smaller space. Just imagine trying to force an entire brick into a thimble!

The only thing powerful enough to force the plutonium sample into a space small enough for the nuclear reaction to work was another bomb—a chemical bomb. The scientists had to build a chemical bomb that would be perfectly controlled so that the shock waves of an explosion hit the plutonium evenly from every direction. They knew that creating such a controlled blast was practically impossible, but the scientists had to try to do it. They had no choice.

THE FIRST USE OF NUCLEAR WEAPONS

After a year of ideas and tests and failures and modifications, the scientists succeeded. Designing and building the plutonium bomb had taken so long that the war with Germany was over before the bomb was ready. The United States was still fighting with Japan, though. The Japanese were losing, but the United States was fairly sure that the Japanese would not surrender until the United States invaded Japan by land. Then, hundreds of thousands of Americans and Japanese would probably die before the war was brought to an end.

President Harry Truman, military leaders, and Los Alamos scientists met to discuss whether nuclear bombs should be used. They all agreed that the quickest way to end the war would be to drop nuclear bombs on two cities in Japan.

On August 6, 1945, two U. S. Army planes flew over Hiroshima. Two days earlier, 720,000 leaflets had been dropped to warn the city that it would be destroyed. But when the citizens of Hiroshima saw only two planes flying overhead, they didn't even head for their bomb shelters. At 8:15 A.M., the *Enola Gay*

An American B-52 named Enola Gay *dropped a nuclear bomb on Hiroshima, Japan, on August 6, 1945.*

dropped a uranium fission bomb on Hiroshima. The pilots knew they were carrying a powerful bomb, but they had no idea how intense the blast would be. The explosion leveled the center of the city instantly, destroying about 60,000 buildings.

One survivor described the scene, "My immediate thought was that this was like the hell I had al-

*Most of the buildings in Hiroshima were destroyed and
thousands of people were killed by the nuclear bomb.*

ways read about. I had never seen anything which re-
sembled it before. But I thought that should there be
a hell, this was it." Many of those who were not
killed by the blast died later of radiation sickness.
When the bomb exploded, radioactivity had rained
down on the city. No one knows exactly how many

people were killed by the bomb; estimates range from 78,000 to 200,000.

On August 9, a plutonium bomb was dropped on Nagasaki, destroying that town as well. On August 14, the Japanese surrendered, and World War II was over.

A BIGGER, BETTER BOMB

Robert and Ernest reacted very differently when they learned how much damage the bombs had caused. Robert, who became known as the father of the atomic bomb, became very depressed. He knew that he had helped create a terrible weapon. He resigned from Los Alamos, and refused to return to Berkeley.

In 1947, he became a professor at Princeton University. He also became an adviser to a subcommittee of the Atomic Energy Commission, which helped the government make decisions related to nuclear arms policy. Robert wanted to make sure that nuclear weapons would never be used again. He knew that other countries would soon figure out how to build plutonium bombs. He hoped that if the United States stopped building bombs, then other countries would stop, too. He tried to convince the United States government of this, but he never succeeded.

Ernest, on the other hand, was not as upset as Robert. He was quick to defend the decision to use the bombs. Of course, Ernest didn't want to see nuclear bombs used again—he just had a different idea of how to achieve this goal. He believed that the United States had to continue researching and building better bombs, so that they would always remain more powerful than other countries. Only then could the United

Robert Oppenheimer at Princeton University

States have enough authority in world affairs to make sure that a nuclear war did not happen.

For the first time since Robert Oppenheimer first came to Berkeley, he and Ernest Lawrence were on opposite sides of the fence. Their friendship, which was already strained, was about to end.

Ernest wanted to start work on a new particle accelerator that would produce plutonium. To build it, he needed federal funding. Robert thought that there were better ways to produce plutonium. As an adviser to a congressional subcommittee, he recommended that funding for Ernest's accelerator be considered a low priority. Ernest was furious. He never spoke to Robert again.

Ernest kept working on his new accelerator, though. He began to build it in a town called Livermore, 60 miles (97 km) from Berkeley. Today Lawrence Livermore Lab is a very prestigious research center. For the first time, Ernest's hard work was not rewarded. After working for 2 hours, the accelerator malfunctioned and never worked again.

Despite this failure, Ernest was determined to participate in weapons research. He teamed up with Edward Teller (the physicist who had problems getting along with Robert at Los Alamos). The two scientists began working on a whole new kind of nuclear bomb, which they nicknamed the Super. This bomb did not rely on fission at all. It did not create an explosion by splitting atoms apart. Much like the sun, it created energy by forcing atoms together in a process called *fusion*. Ernest and Edward claimed it would be even more powerful than a plutonium bomb.

Robert didn't want to see the Super built. He wasn't sure it would work, and he didn't want the United States to create a weapon that was even more deadly than those built at Los Alamos. He advised Congress not to fund the project.

By this time, however, the legislature was less easily influenced by Robert. The Soviet Union now had their own plutonium bomb, and the United States was worried. Congress was convinced that they had to stay one step ahead of the Soviets. Congress voted to

In 1946, Ernest Lawrence received the Civilian Medal of Merit for his part in the development of the atomic bomb.

support Ernest's project, and President Truman held a press conference to announce the plan to the American public.

Over the next few years, Teller and another scientist, Stanislaw Ulam, finalized the design for Super, and they built the bomb. On November 1, 1952, they tested it on a small island in the Pacific Ocean. The new bomb was 500 times more powerful than the uranium bomb dropped on Hiroshima. It produced a 3-mile (4.8-km)-wide fireball that obliterated the island, leaving behind only an underwater crater 200 feet (61 m) deep and 1 mile (1.6 km) across.

In December of 1953, the government revoked Robert Oppenheimer's security clearance. The government had stopped trusting his judgment. Just about everyone in the country believed that the Soviet Union was our greatest enemy, and it was no secret that Robert and his wife had once been involved with Communist organizations. Some members of Congress feared that Robert might not have his nation's best interests in mind, and they no longer wanted to hear his opinions. The man who had been in charge of Los Alamos—one of the most secret projects in United States history—no longer had access to anything confidential.

When a hearing was held to decide whether Robert should get his security clearance back, Ernest Lawrence and Edward Teller were both called as witnesses. Many people believe that Teller's testimony secured the case against Robert.

"Do you or do you not believe that Dr. Oppenheimer is a security risk?" Edward Teller was asked. He gave a carefully worded answer.

In a great number of cases I have seen Dr. Oppenheimer act . . . in a way that is . . . exceedingly hard to understand. I thoroughly disagreed with him on numerous issues and his actions frankly appeared to me confused and complicated. To this extent, I feel that I would like to see the vital interests of this country in hands which I understand better and, therefore, trust more.

As Edward walked out of the courtroom, he stuck out his hand to Robert and said, "I'm sorry."

Robert shook Edward's hand and responded, "After what you've just said, I don't know what you mean."

Robert's security clearance was not reinstated. He wasn't even allowed to read classified papers that he had written himself!

After the hearing, Edward Teller went back to work—only to discover that most of the scientific community had turned against him. They couldn't believe that he would speak out against another scientist so publicly.

ERNEST AND ROBERT: THEIR LAST YEARS

Ernest Lawrence never had an opportunity to testify. On his way to the hearing, he became very sick and had to return home. His health continued to decline for the next few years. On August 27, 1958, Ernest died of internal bleeding. He was 57 years old. After Ernest's death, the United States government created the Lawrence Award, in his honor.

For the next 9 years, Robert Oppenheimer taught and did physics research at Princeton. Nothing he worked on these last years was related to nuclear bombs. On February 18, 1967, he died of throat cancer. He was 62 years old.

Nuclear science was born in Europe. But in the 1930s and 1940s, American science came into its own.

American scientists had an advantage over their European counterparts—both the government and industrial leaders willingly invested in nuclear science research.

By the end of World War II, a whole new era in scientific research had been born. No longer was all research done in small university labs or on shoestring budgets. Big questions needed big experiments and big programs to fund them. Ernest O. Lawrence started the trend when he invented the cyclotron. That effort was soon followed by the even more expansive Manhattan Project led by Robert Oppenheimer. These two men brought scientific research to a whole new level.

FIVE "BRIGHTER THAN ANY GIRL I'D EVER MET"

Maria Goeppert-Mayer and
the Dance of Magic Numbers

2, 8, 20, 28, 50, 82, 126 . . . The numbers danced around in Maria Goeppert-Mayer's head. They didn't make sense. They didn't seem to fit any pattern. Nothing seemed to connect them. There was no reason that these numbers should be important, except that atoms with 2, 8, 20, 28, 50, 82, or 126 neutrons and protons were never radioactive.

Other scientists laughed at Maria. It was 1948, and most of them believed that the nucleus was a tiny drop of liquid filled with neutrons and protons that randomly moved around and sometimes bumped into one another. In radioactive atoms, for some reason, particles were shot out of this liquid nucleus. No one knew why some elements were radioactive and some were not, but they didn't think that Maria's numbers could provide a solution.

Maria didn't think the nucleus of an atom looked like a drop of liquid. She thought that the neutrons and protons moved around in fixed paths. She compared neutrons and protons to dancers waltzing around a room.

She believed that every atom, like every dance hall, could be occupied by the perfect number of dancers. When a dance hall has the perfect number of dancers, no couples get squeezed out and no extra couples can squeeze in. Similarly, an atom with the perfect number of neutrons and protons would neither lose nor gain material. This meant that such atoms would never be radioactive.

Maria thought that her magic numbers might be the equivalent of the perfect number of dancers. This is why she tried desperately to find a pattern among them. She was unable to come up with mathematical equations to prove that her magic numbers represented the perfect number of protons and neutrons. Her magic numbers just didn't make sense.

Then, one day, she was describing her frustration to Enrico Fermi, one of her colleagues at the University of Chicago. Someone interrupted their conversation to tell Enrico that he had received a phone call. As he was leaving the room, he looked over his shoulder and asked a question, "Is there any evidence of spin-orbit coupling?"

Maria felt the excitement shoot through her entire body. She had a physical reaction, an awesome sensation that she was never completely able to describe.

He was already gone when she replied, "Yes, Enrico. That's it."

Maria knew immediately that if she included this last rule about how particles move to her equations, they would work. She began to scribble on a piece of paper. By the time Enrico returned 10 minutes later, she had worked it all out. Enrico knew Maria's the-

Maria Goeppert-Mayer

ory was right. He taught it to his class the very next week.

It had been 37 years since the nucleus was discovered. Scientists had figured out what it was made of, how to make it produce energy, and how to turn it into a bomb. But no one really knew what it looked like, and no one knew why it fissioned or why some nuclei emitted radioactive rays and others did not. These were the problems Maria helped solve.

Young Maria Goeppert-Mayer

Maria Gertrud Käte Goeppert was born on June 28, 1906, to Friedrich and Maria Goeppert. She was born in Kattowitz, a town that was then considered part of

Germany and is now part of Poland. She was brought up in Göttingen because her father was a professor of pediatrics there. Friedrich Goeppert was the sixth in an unbroken line of university professors. He wanted his only child, Maria, to be a professor, too.

The Goeppert household was wealthy. Maria's mother was known for throwing the best parties in town. That changed when World War I began. Everyone in Europe was affected by the war, and Germany was hit especially hard. By the end of the war, Maria's family was eating turnip soup seasoned with pig's ears. Maria later said, "I do not eat turnips to this day. I also do not eat pig's ears."

Very few women went to college in the early 1900s. But Maria was accepted at the University of Göttingen and began to take classes. Even though there were few women on campus, Maria felt right at home. Because her father was a professor at the university, she had spent quite a bit of time there as a child.

Maria was at Göttingen during a period that was very exciting for anyone interested in science. The best physicists in the world came to Göttingen to hammer out the laws of *quantum mechanics*—a branch of physics that deals with the tiny particles inside the nucleus. According to the laws of quantum mechanics, the particles that make up the nucleus of an atom follow different laws of motion than other objects on Earth. After taking a course in quantum mechanics, Maria knew she wanted to be a physicist.

Many of the scientists who attended Göttingen with Maria went on to become world-famous—Enrico Fermi, Edward Teller, and Robert Oppenheimer, to name just a few. Maria had been one of the students annoyed by Robert Oppenheimer's unusual behavior.

Like many other students, she was impressed by his intelligence, but aggravated by his habit of interrupting lectures to explain how something could be done better. Finally, she wrote a letter to one of her professors. She wanted the professor to ask Robert to keep his thoughts to himself.

MARIA GOEPPERT-MAYER MARRIES AND MOVES TO THE UNITED STATES

Another student who Maria noticed was Joseph Mayer, an American who came to Göttingen to study chemistry. Joe noticed Maria, too, and fell in love with her almost immediately. He told a friend she was "brighter than any girl [he] had ever met." Maria was also considered one of the prettiest girls on campus.

Maria didn't fall in love with Joe quite as quickly. She knew that marrying an American would mean that she would have to leave Germany. She would miss her family and friends terribly. Eventually, however, Joe won Maria's heart, and the two were married on January 18, 1930.

During the engagement Maria had stopped working on her dissertation. It looked like she might not receive her Ph.D. Both Joe and Maria's mother were determined to see her become a scientist. Finally, Joe found a way to make Maria return to the lab. When they were planning a large dinner party, Maria became frustrated with all the work involved. In her parents' house, servants had always taken care of the entertaining. Joe told Maria that unless she finished her thesis, she'd better get used to this type of work. He said they could never afford a housekeeper unless she earned her Ph.D. and found a job. Within 4 months, Maria's thesis was finished.

By the time Maria graduated, she was ready to be a professor. There were very few female professors in Germany, but she and Joe were moving to the United States. Maria thought she'd be able to get a job there. Unfortunately, she was wrong about that.

Joe was hired as a professor at Johns Hopkins University in Baltimore. But Johns Hopkins wouldn't hire Maria, even though she had a stronger background in quantum mechanics than anyone on their staff. The school had a policy stating that both members of a married couple could not be professors there. She had trouble finding work elsewhere, too. The Great Depression was just beginning and jobs were scarce. Many employers thought that if a position opened up, it should go to a man who needed to support a family, not a woman whose husband already had a good job.

Eventually, Johns Hopkins begrudgingly agreed to give her an office in an attic. They let her do research as long as she didn't get in the way. Despite these hardships, Maria managed to write numerous scientific papers during the 9 years she lived in Baltimore.

Adjusting to the United States was difficult for Maria. She arrived during Prohibition—when selling, buying, and drinking alcohol were illegal. Maria had been a party girl in Germany. She was used to smoking, drinking, and hosting large dinner parties. She couldn't understand why any country would outlaw alcohol.

Maria often daydreamed about the Germany she had known as a child. But that Germany no longer existed. In the mid1930s, Adolf Hitler rose to power. Maria did not like what he was doing to her beloved homeland. She grew to hate the Nazis.

Many German scientists agreed with Maria. Many of them fled to other countries, including the United States. The Mayer home was often their first stop off the boat. The German refugees stayed with Maria and Joe while they looked for a permanent home. So many people took advantage of the Mayers' hospitality that Maria once received a thank-you note from a man she didn't even remember meeting.

MARIA BECOMES INTERESTED IN NUCLEAR PHYSICS

Eventually, Johns Hopkins began to understand the importance of quantum mechanics and gave Maria more responsibility. Although the school still refused to pay her, the head of the Physics Department asked her to give lectures. She even had a graduate student, Robert Sachs, to assist her.

It was Robert Sachs who first sparked Maria's interest in nuclear physics. He was looking for a thesis topic, and Maria told him that nuclear science was the only field a young theorist should go into. She admitted that she didn't know much about nuclear science, but offered to introduce Robert to someone who did. A few days later, they visited Edward Teller. Edward suggested that Robert write his dissertation on the spins of atomic nuclei.

The particles found inside an atomic nucleus are constantly in motion. Scientists say they are spinning. Just as electrons and protons have different charges, particles in the nucleus have different spins. Some particles spin to the left, while others spin to the right. As a particle spins, it creates a tiny magnetic field around itself. When the spins of all the particles in all the atoms that make up an object are perfectly aligned, a noticeable magnetic field exists around the object. This is why some metals, such as iron, are magnetic.

JOE AND MARIA GO TO NEW YORK

In 1938, Johns Hopkins decided to reorganize the Physics Department to save money. That meant firing the older, higher-paid professors and replacing them with younger, less prominent scientists who would accept lower salaries. Joe Mayer was one of the professors to lose his position. Maria felt she was to blame. She thought the university was tired of making room for her. For the rest of her life, she was reluctant to demand personal recognition.

Leaving Johns Hopkins did not turn out to be a setback for Joe and Maria, however. Joe was soon hired by Columbia University in New York at twice his previous salary. Maria, of course, was not hired. She tried to participate in the department as she had at Johns Hopkins, but the school wanted nothing to do with her. She was even asked not to attend dinners given after the weekly physics seminars!

Some people did make Maria feel welcome, though. The Mayers had arrived in New York just months after the Fermi family. The Fermis, the Mayers, and a third couple, Harold Urey and his wife, became close friends. Enrico and Harold convinced the university that Maria should be allowed to teach some chemistry classes.

During this time, Maria and Joe co-wrote a textbook called *Statistical Mechanics.* It received excellent reviews and became the new standard text. Along with the book, came other forms of recognition. In November of 1940, Maria was elected a Fellow of the American Physical Society. The notification letter sent to her began "Dear Sir."

Two weeks later she was offered her first paid teaching position. She was hired as a math and physics professor by Sarah Lawrence College, an all-women's college in New York. During the interview for this job, a professor asked her if she really thought that teaching girls science was as important as teaching them how to regulate a furnace flue. Maria was stunned. She responded by asking if the only reason girls should learn English was to read a cookbook. It turned out to be the perfect answer. The administration at Sarah Lawrence was just testing Maria to see if she was traditional and dull. She clearly wasn't. The administrator hired Maria on the spot.

Suddenly, Maria's life became very busy. She was teaching full-time at Sarah Lawrence when World War II began. Then Enrico Fermi moved to Chicago to work for the government, and Maria was given 24 hours notice to take over his courses at Columbia.

Next, Harold Urey asked her to help him with some secret work he was doing for the government. Maria didn't know what the big secret was all about, but she didn't want to give up an opportunity to do research. She was concerned, though. She was afraid that she wouldn't have enough time to do research and take care of her family. She agreed to work with Harold, but told him she would not be able to work on Saturdays or when her children were sick.

Harold agreed. For the first time, Maria was doing professional scientific research. "Suddenly I was taken seriously, considered a good scientist," she said later. "It was the beginning of my . . . standing on my own two feet as a scientist."

Maria's research project involved developing a technique for purifying uranium. Because the project was classified, she couldn't tell Joe anything. It was the only time she kept a secret from him. Later, she said that it was one of the hardest things she ever had to do. Maria was also upset about working on something as dangerous and powerful as a nuclear bomb. In the back of her mind, she sometimes hoped it wouldn't work.

Maria was, of course, somewhat torn between her loyalty to the United States and her feelings for Germany, where she still had friends and family. One thing was crystal clear to Maria, Hitler must be stopped. Maria hoped the United States would have a nuclear bomb before Germany.

In the summer of 1945, the Mayer family was on vacation in Nantucket, an island off the coast of Massachusetts. Joe and Maria were walking on the beach when they saw a neighbor running toward them. He told them that there had been a report on the radio announcing that the United States had dropped a bomb on Hiroshima.

The neighbor, who knew that the Mayers were scientists, asked Joe if he'd helped build the bomb. Joe said he hadn't. Maria realized that, at last, she was free to tell her secret. When the neighbor left, she told Joe everything.

*L*IFE IN CHICAGO

After the war, Joseph Mayer was invited to become a professor at the University of Chicago's newly formed Institute for Nuclear Studies, which is now known as the Fermi Institute. Maria was invited to be a volun-

Many of the scientists involved in the effort to develop the nuclear bomb assembled at the University of Chicago's Institute for Nuclear Studies on September 2, 1945. The group included Harold Urey (bottom, second from left); Enrico Fermi (bottom, second from right); Edward Teller (top, left) ; and Joseph Mayer (top, third from right).

tary associate professor. Even though she was not offered a salary, Maria was excited that they wanted her to contribute. They wanted her to teach and do research. "It was the first place where I was not considered a nuisance, but greeted with open arms," said Maria.

Maria never had a great reputation as a professor. She spoke quickly and technically, and refused to liven up her classes with any showmanship. Nevertheless, she attracted many students to her classroom. According to one student who greatly admired Maria:

> Professor Mayer taught solid, no-nonsense courses. . . She was a dedicated cigarette smoker, and in those days, it was quite acceptable for the professor to smoke in class. She often did. She would light up and lecture with a cigarette in one hand, a piece of chalk in the other. She puffed on the one and wrote on the blackboard with the other. They interchanged places in her hands frequently, and in a seemingly random manner. Often in the excitement . . . she would come very, very close to writing with the cigarette or puffing on the chalk.

Robert Sachs, her first graduate student, was also in Chicago. He had continued his studies in nuclear science and was now the director of a new research facility called Argonne National Laboratory. He offered Maria a paying job as a part-time researcher. It was a great opportunity for her. Not only would she earn money, she would have an opportunity to learn more about nuclear physics.

Maria began attending weekly seminars at the Institute for Nuclear Studies. At first, she didn't understand most of the lectures. She didn't want to be a nuisance, so she allowed herself to ask only two questions at each seminar. Even with this limitation, she learned quickly.

She soon discovered that no one understood why some elements are stable and others aren't. Why do some elements stay the same for millennia, while others emit radiation and transform into different elements? This was a key question. Researchers knew the answer lay in the nucleus. They thought that if they could figure out how protons and neutrons are arranged, they might find the answers they were looking for. It was Maria, the newcomer to the field, who did this.

As she taught herself about the nucleus—reading all the papers that scientists had published, she noticed her magic numbers. It took more than a year, and a little nudge from Enrico Fermi, to understand their significance.

Maria was excited, but she could not bring herself to publish her work. She did not want to draw too much attention to herself. Joseph badgered and bothered her until she finally began to write. Maria finished her paper in December of 1949. Around the same time, three other German physicists made the same discovery. When Maria read their paper, she was distressed. She worried that she had not been the first person to understand the nucleus. That feeling lasted only a few moments. Then, she realized that their paper proved that she was right.

She and Hans Jensen, one of the authors of the German paper, decided to write a book that explained their theory to the world. They met in 1951 when the Mayers went to Germany. It was the first time Joe and Maria had been there since World War II. Maria and Hans hit it off immediately. They had a lot in common. In fact, they even wore the same prescription glasses. Their book, *Elementary Theory of Nuclear Shell Structure,* was published in 1955.

The Mayers continued working at Chicago for several more years. In 1959, both were invited to become professors at the University of California in San Diego. This was the first time Maria, now 53 years old, was offered a paying job as a full-time professor.

The next day, the University of Chicago also offered Maria a salary. The school didn't want her to leave. But it was too little, too late. The Mayers moved to California, and Maria finally fulfilled her father's wish of becoming a professor.

Shortly after the Mayer family arrived in San Diego, Maria had a stroke. She kept working, but was never completely healthy again.

At 4:00 A.M. on November 5, 1963, the phone rang in the Mayers' home. When Joe answered, the operator told him there was a call for Maria from Stockholm. He handed her the phone. As she sleepily said,

Maria Goeppert-Mayer (center) and Hans Jensen (right) look on as Eugene Wigner (right, on podium) is awarded the Nobel Prize for physics in 1963. All three scientists won Nobel Prizes that year.

"But I don't know anyone in Stockholm," Joe ran into the kitchen to put some champagne on ice.

The call notified Maria that she and Hans Jensen had won the 1963 Nobel Prize for physics for their discovery of the nuclear shell model. She became the third woman to win a Nobel Prize in the sciences. To this day, she and Marie Curie are the only two women to win a Nobel Prize in physics.

That December, as she sat on the platform to receive her prize, Joe sat below her in the audience. He was so proud of her that tears streamed down his face. "La Jolla Mother Wins Nobel Prize" was one of the local headlines announcing Maria's victory. This was typical of the recognition she received as a female scientist. She was always identified as a woman first, and a great scientist second.

During the next 6 years, the Mayers continued their work, but Maria's health declined rapidly. On February 20, 1972, at the age of 66, Maria died of a heart attack.

SIX "THE CENTER OF A GREAT ENTERPRISE"

Andrei Sakharov Creates the Hydrogen Bomb

*W*orld politics changed after the United States built the first nuclear bombs. Relations between the United States and the Soviet Union became strained. The Soviet Union was afraid that nuclear weapons gave the United States too much power, so they brought a group of scientists to a top-secret site—a compound called the Installation—and asked them to build a weapon more powerful than the plutonium bomb.

Andrei Sakharov, one of the stars of Soviet nuclear science, lived behind the Installation's barbed-wire fence for 18 years. The fence was meant to keep the public out and the scientists in. Andrei and his colleagues were investigating how to make a *hydrogen bomb* that relied on fusion like Edward Teller's Super bomb.

On November 22, 1955, Andrei watched the first test of the bomb he had helped build. The light given off by a hydrogen bomb is so bright that it can blind you. So even though Andrei watched from miles away, he stood with his back to the bomb and turned around just after it went off.

An enormous sphere of yellow light began to swell. As it grew, it turned from orange to yellow to bright red. Soon the light filled the horizon. Next, a monstrous swirling cloud of dust rose into the sky. The dust spread out to form a mushroom. Andrei felt a burst of heat on his face. Even though it was the middle of winter and he was miles away from the explosion site, he felt as if he had just stepped in front of an open furnace.

The Soviet Union's first attempt to create a hydrogen bomb was successful. The scientists rejoiced. They believed that as long as the Soviet Union had nuclear weapons, their nation would be as powerful as their enemy—the United States. This was not the only reason the scientists were so happy. They knew that if the test had failed, the government would have been very angry. The scientists might have been put in jail, or even executed.

But Andrei was also worried about the bomb's success. He knew how deadly the hydrogen bomb was, and he didn't want to see it used in war. At a celebration the night of the test, Andrei raised his wine glass to toast his comrades, "May all our devices explode as successfully as today's," he said. "But always over test sites and never over cities."

The room fell silent. No one could believe that Andrei would make such a statement publicly. This episode was a sign of things to come. Over the years, Andrei would become more and more outspoken against the Soviet government. Eventually, he was forced into exile.

YOUNG ANDREI SAKHAROV

Andrei Sakharov was born in Moscow on May 21, 1921, to Ekaterina and Nikolai Sakharov. The family lived in one room of an apartment that housed six families.

The 1920s and 1930s were hard in the Soviet Union. There was a brand-new Communist government and the people were full of hope. Would life be better for everyone? It wasn't. Nevertheless, Andrei grew up believing the Communist government was generally good for the Russian people.

Andrei's father, a physics professor, often showed his son the experiments he was teaching his students. Andrei thought that they were like magic tricks. He decided that he wanted to be a physicist, too. In Andrei's third year of college, however, he was forced to put his plans on hold.

It was June of 1941, and the Russians were pulled into World War II. Andrei finished college, but he couldn't go on to graduate school while there was a war going on. Instead, he went to work for a company that built weapon parts and ammunition. He invented several tools, and received a patent for one that tested the quality of steel bullets. This was Andrei's first opportunity to work with physics.

In 1942, he met a woman named Klava. They were married on July 10, 1943, exactly 8 months after they met. Andrei spent the rest of the war working in the ammunitions plant during the day and studying physics at night. He read book after book, and even wrote a few papers.

Andrei was relieved when Germany surrendered to the Allies in May of 1945. He knew the Americans were still fighting the Japanese, but for him—and his nation—the war was over. When the United States dropped an atomic bomb on Hiroshima in August, Andrei said, "I was so stunned that my legs practically gave way. There could be no doubt that my fate and the fate of many others, perhaps of the entire world, had changed overnight."

$\mathcal{L}$IFE AFTER THE WAR

When the war was over, Andrei decided that the life of an inventor didn't suit him. He wanted to fulfill his dream of getting a doctorate in physics. He applied to school at FIAN (the Physics Institute of the Academy of Sciences) in Moscow and interviewed with Igor Tamm, a physicist who won the Nobel Prize in 1958. Although much of the physics that Andrei knew was self-taught, Igor was impressed. But there was a problem—Andrei didn't know English. Igor was appalled by this.

He accepted accepted Andrei into graduate school, but said, "You've got to learn English right away. Without English you can't even get started, and you'll never get anywhere."

The next few years were tough on the Sakharov family. After the war ended, it was difficult for people in the Soviet Union to get enough food or find a place to live. No one lived in apartments by themselves; several families had to share a few rooms. And for several years, they never stayed in one place for more than 2 months.

They were kicked out of one apartment when a *KGB* agent approached Klava and asked her to spy on her husband. He said it was part of the routine KGB surveillance of all Russian citizens. Klava refused, and the Soviet government had the Sakharovs evicted.

Apart from the economic problems facing all soviet citizens, Andrei enjoyed the years he spent in graduate school. He taught a nuclear science course that covered everything scientists had learned before World War II. After that point, scientists had stopped publishing their results.

What his students didn't know was that Andrei was learning the details of nuclear science at the same time as he was teaching them. As a result, it took him at least a day to prepare each of his 2-hour lectures. After teaching, he was often so tired that he couldn't work on his own research. But, in the end, the experience helped him to thoroughly understand nuclear science. He wrote in his memoirs, "I often think how wonderful it would have been if I'd had the time to go through all the disciplines of theoretical physics that way."

Andrei did not teach his students about chain reactions. He knew that uranium could fission, since that research was done just before the war, but he did not yet realize how the energy from fission could be used.

ANDREI SAKHAROV GOES TO WORK FOR THE GOVERNMENT

The Soviet government knew that Andrei was a good nuclear scientist, and they wanted him to work for them. Twice, Russian officials asked Andrei to leave FIAN to do nuclear research for the government, and twice Andrei refused. They didn't ask him a third time—they ordered him. Both Andrei and Igor Tamm were required to join a government group that was

*Andrei Sakharov
as a young man*

studying how to build nuclear weapons. That is how the Sakharov family ended up at the Installation.

Not only was Andrei forbidden to leave the compound without permission, he couldn't even leave his house without notifying his two bodyguards! The bodyguards spent as much time spying on Andrei as they did protecting him, but Andrei was so caught up in the project that he didn't really notice the restrictions. "We saw ourselves at the center of a great enterprise," he said. "We never questioned the vital importance of the work."

The scientists at the Installation had to take an oath not to discuss their research or reveal government secrets. Andrei kept his word. Even when he began fighting with the Soviet government, Andrei never went back on his promise. Nevertheless, some of the stories of what happened inside the Installation have been exposed. The Soviets found a relatively easy way to build a plutonium bomb—they got their information from spies in the United States.

This information was not enough to satisfy the Soviets. They knew that Edward Teller and Stanislaw Ulam were working on the Super A-bomb. The Soviet government wanted to build a bomb just as powerful. Since the two nations were working on this project at the same time, the Soviets couldn't just copy the American version. Andrei and his colleagues had to figure out how to build the new bomb on their own.

Andrei knew that fusion was almost the exact opposite of fission. Two atoms are forced together into one, instead of one splitting into two. When this happens, a huge amount of energy is released. Where does all that energy come from? For example, if two hydrogen atoms—each with just one proton in its nucleus—fuse, they form a helium atom with two protons. The mass of a single helium atom is less than the combined mass of two hydrogen atoms. This means that during fusion, some material—or matter—seems to vanish. But, actually, it doesn't disappear—it is converted into energy.

How do scientists know this? The total amount of matter plus energy in the universe does not change, but matter can be converted into energy and energy can be converted into matter. In cases where matter seems to be lost, it is really converted into energy.

Andrei also knew that energy from fusion is what keeps the sun burning. More than 75 percent of the sun is made of hydrogen. Deep in the heart of the star, hydrogen atoms are constantly fusing to form heavier elements. Each second, the sun converts 700 million tons of hydrogen to heavier elements. The sun's heat and light energy are also produced as the atoms fuse. Without fusion, there would be no life on Earth.

Fusion occurs naturally only at extremely high temperatures. The temperature at the center of the sun reaches about 27 million °F (15 million °C). If Andrei wanted to build a fusion bomb, first he had to figure out how to create that much heat on Earth. At first, he thought it might be possible to create the heat necessary for fusion using a fission bomb. Today, many people don't consider this type of bomb to be a true fusion bomb because it relies more on fission than fusion. But that doesn't mean that Andrei's bomb wasn't incredibly destructive.

The Russians tested this bomb, which the United States called Joe 4, in August of 1953. After the test, the head of the KGB gave awards to the scientists who had worked on the project. It is said that the prize each scientist received was based on how severe his punishment would have been if the test had failed. In other words, those who would have been shot were awarded the highest prize—the Hero of Socialist Labor—while those who would have received extended prison sentences received the Order of Lenin. Andrei Sakharov received the Hero of Socialist Labor award.

During the next 10 years, Andrei won the award two more times. He won the prize again because he went right back to work as soon as the test was over. His new goal was to build an even more powerful nuclear bomb. The Soviets didn't want to just keep pace with American bomb research, they wanted to surpass it.

Andrei quickly realized that to build a more deadly bomb, the scientists would have to completely revise their design. Instead of relying on a fission bomb to generate heat, they tried putting the fusion bomb under intense pressure. They imploded (forced together) the hydrogen core of the fusion bomb just as they imploded the plutonium in a fission bomb. After implosion, the core was 1,000 times denser than it had been just microseconds earlier.

Because a material gets hotter when it gets denser, forcing all the atoms together heated the hydrogen enough to set off a fusion reaction. This scheme became the basic blueprint used to build all future fusion bombs. In the United States, Edward Teller and Stanislaw Ulam had come up with the same design. As a result, this kind of thermonuclear weapon is known as the Teller-Ulam configuration.

Beyond the Bomb

Andrei didn't spend all his time working on bombs. He wanted to find out if it would be possible to use fusion to produce energy for nuclear power plants. Just as Enrico Fermi had invented a way to produce a controlled release of energy to create electricity, Andrei wanted to produce controlled energy from fusion. Fusion would be better than fission for two reasons—it could produce more energy than fission and it could harness energy from cheap materials, such as hydrogen, as opposed to expensive ones, such as plutonium.

In addition, energy from fusion is much cleaner. Because fission gives off radioactivity, nuclear fission reactors must be built very carefully to make sure that radioactivity doesn't leak. Despite the precautions taken, accidents have happened, and many people worry that nuclear energy from fission is not safe. A fusion reactor would produce more energy and much less radioactivity.

The biggest problem with building a fusion reactor is the same as the problem with building a fusion bomb—creating enough heat to initiate the process. Even if this were possible, how could something that hot be contained? Any container made of synthetic materials would melt instantly.

Andrei tried to tackle this problem. He considered a setup that involved suspending hydrogen in midair with magnets. If the hydrogen floated, Andrei reasoned, it wouldn't touch the walls of its container and, therefore, couldn't burn them. Some people still use Andrei's technique today in their quest to get energy from fusion. But even now, no one can build a fusion reactor powerful enough to be useful.

During his years at the Installation, Andrei also studied the dangers of exposure to nuclear bombs. He wondered how the radiation would affect people who were bombed, but he was also interested in the effect it might have on people who lived near test sites. Bombs were tested in deserted areas and, although they did not kill anyone directly, they did send radioactive substances into the atmosphere.

In March of 1954, the United States tested a hydrogen bomb on a small, deserted island in the Pacific Ocean. It was quite windy on the day of the test, and clouds of radioactivity spread over five or six neighboring islands. All the inhabitants had to be evacuated.

Creatures on Earth are exposed to radiation every single day. Radiation comes in the form of cosmic and ultraviolet rays that stream down on us from the sun. It is also released by uranium and other elements found in the earth. Under normal circumstances, these forms of "natural radiation" do not seem to be deadly. Yet, ever since the time of the Curies, people have known that exposure to high levels of radiation can damage the cells of living things. In some cases, the damage is severe enough to cause disease, or even death. Andrei believed that the radiation being added to the air by tests conducted by the United States, the Soviet Union, and Great Britain could be hazardous to everyone, especially people living near test sites.

It is difficult to determine the harmful effects of radiation. After all, radiation is not the only cause of cancer or related diseases. How can we determine which ones are the result of radiation exposure? Andrei tried. In 1957, he wrote a paper estimating that for every megaton detonation of a nuclear device, 10,000 people would become ill or die. By the time he wrote the paper, more than 50 megatons of nuclear weapons had been exploded during tests.

Other scientists came up with similar figures. The United States, the Soviet Union, and Great Britain agreed to stop all nuclear testing. Unfortunately, the ban on tests did not last long. In 1961, Nikita Khrushchev, the leader of the Soviet Union, announced to a group of party leaders and atomic scientists that the Soviet Union was going to start testing again. Andrei, who was present when the announcement was made, quickly passed the Soviet leader a note saying that he thought renewed testing was a bad idea. The Soviet leader read the note in silence and put it in his pocket. Later in the evening, he waved the note at the crowd and made fun of Andrei.

"Leave politics to us; we're the specialists," Nikita Khrushchev said. "You make your bombs and test them, and we won't interfere with you. . . . Don't try to tell us what to do or how to behave. We understand politics. I'd be a jellyfish and not chairman of the Council of Ministers if I listened to people like Sakharov."

Nevertheless, the scientists at the Installation were spending less and less time on developing nuclear weapons. This gave Andrei the chance to return to theoretical physics. All over the world, nuclear science was giving way to particle physics. The nucleus that Ernest Rutherford had thought unbelievably small, was now considered big. Physicists spent their time studying neutrons, protons, electrons, and even tinier particles. In the 1960s, scientists discovered that protons and neutrons are made of something even smaller—*quarks*.

DELVING INTO PARTICLE PHYSICS

Andrei became interested in a problem that still confuses scientists today. For a long time, scientists have believed that all the matter in our universe was created moments after the Big Bang. But this idea seems to conflict with something that particle physicists uncovered.

Their research suggests that for every particle in nature, there is an anti-particle. Physicists can create these anti-particles in accelerators. For example, an anti-electron, or *positron,* looks and behaves just like an electron, but its charge is positive instead of negative. When an electron and a positron collide, both particles self-destruct. This happens whenever matter collides with anti-matter.

According to this theory, the Big Bang should have created the same amount of matter and anti-matter. But if that had happened, why didn't all the matter and anti-matter collide and self-destruct? How is it that we have a lot of matter in our universe, but little naturally occurring anti-matter?

In 1967, Andrei wrote one of the most famous physics papers of this century. He suggested that the extremely unusual circumstances of the Big Bang (including phenomenally high temperatures) would make anti-particles and particles behave differently than they do today. If his idea is correct, then, every once in a long while, some protons must spontaneously decay into another particle—in the same way that a radioactive element spontaneously decays into another element, a neutron can change into a proton and an electron.

Although other scientists thought Andrei's theory was brilliant, no one has ever been able to show that protons decay. Nevertheless, the idea makes so much sense that many new theories have been based on it.

A VOICE AGAINST COMMUNISM

As time passed, Andrei began to publicly rebuke the Communist government. In the United States, the right to say what you think is taken for granted. In fact, it is a right guaranteed by the Constitution. But in the Soviet Union, speaking out against the government was illegal.

Andrei believed this law was a violation of human rights. Because Andrei had done so much for the government, he wasn't put on trial, but he was punished. He was demoted from department head at the Installation, and his salary was cut in half. These actions did not discourage Andrei. He had already chosen his path and nothing could throw him off course.

Andrei wrote what was to become one of his most well-known papers. It was not a scientific one. It was entitled "Reflections on Progress, Peaceful Coexistence, and Intellectual Freedom." The essay discussed what Andrei perceived as the greatest threats to the human race, including nuclear war, ecological catastrophe, and famine. He believed that only through merging socialist and capitalist ideas could poverty, prejudice, and war be eliminated. Andrei encouraged the people of the world to work together for these goals.

When Andrei finished writing the paper, he gave it to several friends, and they passed it on to others. Soon copies were circulated throughout Moscow, then all of Russia, and finally in other countries. It was published in a Dutch newspaper. A few weeks later, it was printed in *The New York Times.* Andrei, Klava, and their children were all in Moscow at the time. The government told the Sakharovs that they could not return to the Installation. Andrei had been fired.

FIAN invited Andrei to return and do research in theoretical physics. Andrei agreed. Although he was grateful to be employed, this was a period of great sadness for Andrei. Soon after returning to FIAN, his wife, Klava, died of stomach cancer. Andrei missed her very much. Many people say that after Klava's death, Andrei never approached his scientific work with the same vigor.

Now that Klava was gone, his interest in promoting peace and human rights took center stage. He spoke out against the use of thermonuclear weapons. He began to attend the trials of dissidents he thought had been wrongly accused, and signed letters on their behalf. He also helped launch a Human Rights Committee.

Through his crusades, he met another outspoken supporter of human rights—Elena Bonner. Andrei and Elena—or Lusia, as Andrei called her—were perfectly matched. They fell in love and were married on January 7, 1972. Friends described the couple as incredibly happy. "It was touching to see them constantly holding hands," said one friend. "Not even newlyweds would sit like that."

The couple continued to speak out against the Soviet government. Andrei believed that his status as the creator of the hydrogen bomb would protect him from serious punishment. As the years passed, he and Lusia became more and more outspoken, and eventually, the government retaliated. The KGB began to watch the couple constantly. They received threats against their lives and the lives of their children and grandchildren.

In 1974, Lusia's eyesight began to deteriorate. She needed an operation performed by specialists in Italy. The timing could not have been more perfect. On October 9, 1975, while Lusia was still in Italy, Andrei went to dinner at a friend's house. As they were eating, they heard a knock at the door. A group of journalists had tracked Andrei down to tell him that he had won the Nobel Peace Prize. They videotaped Andrei's reaction.

When Andrei heard the news, he said, "This is a great honor not just for me but for the whole human rights movement. I feel I share this honor with our prisoners of conscience. They have sacrificed their most precious possession—their liberty—in defending others by open and nonviolent means. I hope for an improvement in the lot of political prisoners in the USSR and for a worldwide political amnesty."

Andrei asked the Soviet government for permission to leave the country to accept the prize in person, but he knew he would never be allowed to go. The government had no control over Lusia, though,

Andrei Sakharov in 1975

since she was still in Italy. She flew to Oslo, Norway, and on December 10, 1975, accepted the award on Andrei's behalf. Andrei heard her give the speech on the radio.

In December of 1979, the Soviet Union sent troops into Afghanistan. Andrei spoke out against the invasion. On January 1, 1980, he told a foreign newspaper that he believed the Olympic Committee should refuse to hold the Olympic Games in Moscow that summer if the Soviet Union did not withdraw its troops. Seven days later, *The New York Times* printed what he had said.

Two weeks later, as Andrei was on his way to work, KGB agents stopped his car and took him to a government building. He was told that he was sentenced, without arrest or trial, to internal exile in Siberia. He was forced to live in Gorky and could no longer talk to the media.

Lusia was allowed to live with Andrei, and she could travel back and forth to Moscow—at least for a while. But, when the government discovered that she was carrying messages from Andrei to the press, she was also sentenced to permanent exile in Siberia.

The health of both Andrei and Lusia began to fail while they were in Gorky. Their general health was not helped by their periodic hunger strikes for various causes. Andrei's last hunger strike was an effort to draw attention to the fact that Lusia needed open heart surgery. Eventually, the Soviet government allowed her to travel to the United States for the operation.

Slowly, things were changing in the Soviet Union. A new leader, Mikhail Gorbachev, had risen to power. He was allowing citizens more freedom than they'd experienced since the Communist takeover in 1917.

Eight years after Andrei had been exiled to Siberia, he received a call. It was from Mikhail Gorbachev. The leader of the Soviet Union told Andrei that he and Lusia were free to return to Moscow and continue their patriotic work. Andrei spent his first day in Moscow talking with his colleagues at FIAN. The only people who had been allowed to visit him in Gorky were scientists, so Andrei had a pretty good idea of what had been happening in the world of physics.

Andrei spent the next 2 years promoting human rights. He was elected to the Soviet Congress of People's Deputies, where he finally had more power to affect Soviet policies. On December 14, 1989, just hours after arguing against the Communist Party's monopoly on Soviet politics, Andrei Sakharov died. He was 68 years old.

Andrei Sakharov had always stayed true to his personal beliefs. He was passionate about his physics and passionate about his politics. He sought knowledge and wanted to understand the world. He also realized that knowledge comes with risks. We can use it to destroy as well as to create.

GLOSSARY

alpha ray—a positively charged particle ejected from some radioactive nuclei. Alpha rays are made of two neutrons and two protons, and so are identical to a helium nucleus.

atom—the smallest part of a substance that can exist and still be that substance. An atom consists of a nucleus surrounded by electrons.

atomic weight—the average mass of one atom of an element.

beta ray—a negatively charged, fast-moving particle ejected from some radioactive nuclei. A beta ray is actually a very energetic electron.

chain reaction—a series of events so related that one causes the next. In nuclear physics, it refers to the fact that a fissioning atom can cause another atom to fission.

electron—a negatively charged particle in the atom that moves around the nucleus.

element—a substance that contains only one type of atom. Examples include oxygen, tin, and gold. There are more than 100 known elements—all of which can be found on the periodic table.

Fermi constant—one of the numbers used to calculate the weak force.

fission—when a nucleus splits in two. When a nucleus fissions, it produces energy.

fusion—when two nuclei come together and create a heavier nucleus. This produces even more energy than fission.

half-life—the time required for half of the nuclei to undergo radioactive decay

hydrogen bomb—a bomb that uses fusion. Also referred to as a thermonuclear bomb, or the Super.

ions—atoms that don't have an equal number of electrons and protons. Atoms have no electric charge, but ions are either positively or negatively charged.

KGB—an agency of the former Soviet Union that operated a secret-police force.

matter— anything that has mass and exists as a solid, liquid, or gas.

molecule—a group of atoms that form the smallest unit of a substance that can exist and retain its chemical properties.

neutron—an uncharged particle in the nucleus.

nuclear science—a branch of science that studies the nucleus.

nucleus—made up of protons and neutrons, it sits at the center of an atom.

particle accelerator—an apparatus that speeds charged particles.

periodic table—a chart that shows elements arranged according to their atomic numbers.

positron—the anti-particle of the electron.

proton—a positively charged particle normally found in the nucleus.

quantum mechanics—a field of physics that describes the motion of atomic particles.

quark—one of the group of particles thought to be the basic subunits of neutrons and protons.

radioactive—anything that gives off alpha, beta, or gamma rays. Since these rays can be harmful, prolonged exposure to radioactive substances can be dangerous.

subatomic particles—particles that can be found in the atom. Includes protons, neutrons, and electrons.

weak force—the fundamental physical force responsible for certain kinds of radioactive decay processes.

SELECTED BIBLIOGRAPHY

GENERAL WORKS CONSULTED

Asimov, Isaac. *Asimov's Chronology of Science and Discovery*. New York: HarperCollins, 1994.

Dash, Joan. *The Triumph of Discovery: Women Scientists Who Won the Nobel Prize*. New York: Julian Messner, 1991.

McGrayne, Sharon Bertsch. *Nobel Prize Women in Science: Their Lives, Struggles, and Momentous Discoveries*. New York: Birch Lane Press, 1993.

Weart, Spencer R. and Melba Phillips, Ed. *History of Physics*. Readings from Physics Today 2. New York: American Institute of Physics: 1985.

CHAPTER I

Curie, Eve. *Madame Curie: A Biography*. Trans. Vincent Sheean. New York: Doubleday, Doran and Co., Inc. 1938.

Curie, Marie. *Pierre Curie (with Autobiographical Notes by Marie Curie)*. Trans. Charlotte and Vernon Kellogg. New York: MacMillan Co., 1923.

Pflaum, Rosalynd. *Grand Obsession: Madame Curie and Her World*. New York: Doubleday, 1989.

Quinn, Susan. *Marie Curie: A Life*. Radcliffe Biography Series. New York: Simon & Schuster, 1995.

CHAPTER 2

Eve, A.S. *Rutherford: Being the Life and Letters of the R. Hon. Lord Rutherford, O.M.* Cambridge: Cambridge Press, 1939.

McKown, Robin. *Giant of the Atom: Ernest Rutherford*. New York: Julian Messner, 1962.

Moon, P.B. *Ernest Rutherford and the Atom*. Pioneers of Science and Discovery series. London: Priory Press Limited, 1974.

CHAPTER 3

De Latil, Pierre. *Enrico Fermi: The Man and his Theories*. Trans. Len Ortzen. Profiles in Science series. London: Souvenir Press, 1965.

Fermi, Laura. *Atoms in the Family: My Life with Enrico Fermi* The History of Modern Physics 1800–1950 Vol. 9. 1954. New York: American Institute of Physics, 1987.

Segrè, Emilio. *Enrico Fermi: Physicist*. Chicago: University of Chicago, 1970.

CHAPTER 4

Childs, Herbert. *An American Genius: The Life of*

Ernest Orlando Lawrence. New York: E.P. Dutton & Co., Inc., 1968.

Davis, Nuel Pharr. *Lawrence and Oppenheimer*. New York: Simon and Schuster, 1968.

Goodchild, Peter. *J. Robert Oppenheimer: Shatterer of Worlds*. Boston: Houghton Mifflin Company, 1981.

Michelmore, Peter. *The Swift Years: The J. Robert Oppenheimer Story*. New York: Dodd, Mead & Company, 1969.

CHAPTER 5
Johnson, Karen Elise. *Maria Goeppert-Mayer and the Development of the Nuclear Shell Model*. Diss. U. Minnesota, 1986. Ann Arbor: UMI, 1987. 8625899.

CHAPTER 6
Cochran, Thomas B., Robert S. Norris, and Oleg A. Bukharin. *Making the Russian Bomb: From Stalin to Yeltsin*. Boulder, CO: Westview Press, 1995.

Drell, Sidney D. and Sergei P. Kapitza, Ed. *Sakharov Remembered: A Tribute by Friends and Colleagues*. New York: American Institute of Physics, 1991.

Sakharov, Andrei. *Memoirs*. Trans. Richard Lourie. New York: Alfred A. Knopf, 1990.

INTERNET RESOURCES

A BASIC INTRODUCTION TO NUCLEAR PHYSICS
http://www.scri.fsu.edu/~jac/Nuclear/

The name says it all. This site will help you understand the intricacies of nuclear science. It also describes the types of jobs available in this field and the types of projects that nuclear scientists conduct today.

MARIE CURIE
http://www.xray.hmc.psu.edu/rci/ss4/ss4_11.html

This site has links to sites that describe her life, her research, and the implications her work has had on science and society.

THE *ENOLA GAY* AND THE ATOMIC BOMB
http://www.nhk.or.jp/nuclear/e/text/sumiso.htm

This cyber exhibit developed by the Smithsonian Institution in Washington, D.C., includes information about the war in the Pacific, the decision to drop the bomb, the *Enola Gay*'s mission, Hiroshima and Nagasaki, and the Japanese surrender.

THE MANHATTAN PROJECT
http://www.gis.net/~carter/manhattan/index.html

Learn more about the Manhattan Project. This site describes the personalities, the science, and the political, social, and economic controversies.

NUCLEAR FISSION
http://tqd.advanced.org/3471/fission_body.html

This site provides a complete, comprehensive description of nuclear fission. Links take you to sites that discuss some of the major contributors to this field.

NUCLEAR PHYSICS: PAST, PRESENT, AND FUTURE
http://tqd.advanced.org/3471/

Here's all kinds of general information about the applications of nuclear science and the political controversies surrounding the dangers of using nuclear energy and disposing of nuclear wastes.

INDEX

ABOUT THE AUTHOR

Karen Celia Fox anchors the radio show Science Report for the American Institute of Physics. She majored in physics and English at Amherst College and went on to graduate school in science communication at the University of California, Santa Cruz. She lives in Washington, D.C., and very much wishes she could have met Maria Goeppert-Mayer.